LIVING WITH HOUSEPLANTS

Flowering Plants

TORSTAR BOOKS

NEW YORK · TORONTO

Torstar Books Inc, 41 Madison Avenue, Suite 2900, New York, NY 10010 in collaboration with ICA-förlaget AB, Västerås, Sweden.

© Torstar Books Inc, 1986, except for photographs pp. 1 and 4–63 © ICA-förlaget 1985

Library of Congress Cataloging in Publication Data
Flowering plants.
    (Living with Houseplants)
    Includes index.
    1. House plants.   2. Flowers.
I. Torstar Books (Firm)   II. Series.
SB419.F56 1986   635.9'65   86–11350

ISBN 1–55001–064–6 (Living With Houseplants Series)
ISBN 1–55001–062–X (Flowering Plants)

10 9 8 7 6 5 4 3 2 1
Printed in Belgium

CONTENTS

Flowering maple

ABUTILON HYBRIDUM

The flowering maple (*Abutilon hybridum*) comes from Central and South America but is now a popular, easy-to-care-for houseplant. There are about 150 species in the genus *Abutilon* – an Arabic word for a species of mallow – found in warm and temperate regions of all continents except Europe. Abutilons are members of the Malvaceae family.

The popularity of the flowering maple has encouraged the development of several hybrids with larger-than-normal blossoms in a wide range of colors. *A. hybridum* can reach a height of about 5 feet, with a spread of up to 5 feet, and has maplelike leaves up to 3 inches long.

Even as a young plant it blooms profusely in summer, bearing lantern- or bell-shaped flowers with five papery-thin petals and prominent orange or yellow stamens. Each flower is backed with a pale-green calyx of about an inch long that protects the unopened flower bud.

Other attractive varieties of this plant include 'Boule de Neige', which has white flowers and stamens, 'Golden Fleece', with yellow flowers and 'Master Hugh', with rose-pink blooms.

Sometimes known as the trailing abutilon, *A. megapotamicum* has slender stems and red-and-yellow blossoms with large, dark-brown anthers. It looks particularly attractive in a hanging basket or grown over a trellis. Another interesting plant is

GREEN THUMB GUIDE

Watering and feeding

Water moderately through the active growth period, giving enough to moisten the mixture throughout. Allow the top half-inch of soil to dry out between waterings. In winter, water sparingly, just enough to prevent the soil from drying out. Feed with standard water-soluble fertilizer every two weeks during the period of active growth.

Light and temperature

Abutilons like bright light and at least three to four hours of direct sunlight daily. Poor light makes the plants spindly and weak. Normal room temperatures are suitable but should not fall below 50°F.

Soil and repotting

Use a soil-based mix containing equal parts of sterilized loam soil, peat moss and coarse sand or perlite. Repot in spring to a pot one size larger.

A. pictum 'Thompsonii', which has pretty, variegated leaves and orange-salmon flowers with red veining. The rich mottling of yellow on its dark-green leaves is caused by a harmless virus. This develops when a shoot with the virus is grafted onto a green-leaved plant.

The flowering maple is known for its rapid and vigorous growth but must be pruned regularly to maintain its shape and size. To encourage a bushy appearance, prune shoots in spring and reduce the plant to half its size in fall.

The only pest likely to attack abutilons is the mealy bug. Remove any visible bugs or paint the affected area with denatured alcohol and spray top growth with pesticide.

Most abutilons can be grown from seeds or cuttings, but the variegated form must be grown from cuttings. Select a tip cutting 3 or 4 inches long and dip the cut end in hormone rooting powder to encourage the rooting process. Plant the cutting in a 3- or 4-inch pot containing a mixture of equal parts of moistened peat moss and coarse sand or perlite. Cover the whole pot with a plastic bag to retain the humidity and place it in filtered sunlight. Three to four weeks later the cutting should have rooted and the plastic bag can be removed. Transfer the new plant to a larger pot and treat as a mature plant.

The flowering maple (*Abutilon hybridum*) produces a mass of papery-thin, colorful flowers. Two popular varieties shown here are 'Master Hugh', with deep rose-pink flowers, and 'Golden Fleece', with vivid yellow blooms.

Chenille plant

ACALYPHA HISPIDA

Known as the red-hot cattail or chenille plant, *Acalypha hispida* is grown indoors for its unusual strings of fuzzy red flowers. It is a member of the Euphorbiaceae family and one of over 400 species of acalypha distributed throughout warmer regions of the world – this particular one comes from Papua New Guinea. All are fast-growing plants that need severe cutting back to keep them a manageable size for houseplants.

Of all the acalyphas, *A. hispida* is the most interesting because of its flowers. These fringelike clusters of tiny red blooms can be more than 20 inches long and have a texture similar to the material chenille. The plant's broad oval leaves are slightly hairy and bright green in color. They may be up to 3 inches wide and 5 to 8 inches long. The variety, *A. h.* 'Alba' has cream-white flowers.

Other plants of the genus acalypha have small, rather insignificant flowers and are grown primarily for their attractive foliage. These include *A. wilkesiana*, known as the beefsteak plant, Jacob's coat or match-me-if-you-can. Its striking leaves are coppery-green, mottled and streaked with copper, red and purple. Other varieties with attractive foliage include *A. w.* 'Macrophylla', *A. w.* 'Marginata', *A. w.* 'Musaica' and *A. w.* 'Godseffiana', which has dark-green leaves edged with white.

Acalyphas are at their best when young and, after being used for propagation, usually have to be discarded in their second year. Propagate by taking tip cuttings of 3 to 4 inches long in spring, or by removing short side shoots. If you decide to use the side shoot method, first cut down the old plant to within a foot of the potting mix to encourage new side shoots to appear. Leave them until they grow 3 to 4 inches long, and then, with a sharp downward tug, remove from the parent plant. Make sure that each shoot comes away cleanly with a heel attached.

Place the tip cuttings or side shoots in a 3-inch pot containing a moistened mix of equal parts of peat moss and coarse sand. Cover the whole pot with a plastic bag to keep humidity high, and set it in bright filtered light with a temperature of at least 70°F.

Once there are definite signs of growth, remove the plastic bag and water just enough to keep the potting mix barely moist. Feed with water-soluble fertilizer, diluted to half-strength, every two weeks. When the cuttings or shoots have grown to a height of about 1 foot, move them to 4-inch pots and treat as mature plants.

Acalyphas are vulnerable to red spider mites and mealy bugs. Keep a watch for these pests and mist leaves regularly to discourage them. Treat any infestations that do occur with the appropriate pesticide.

PRUNING ACALYPHA

Prevent an acalypha from becoming straggly by judicious pruning. After the first year's blooms have faded, remove the side shoots. In the second and subsequent years, cut back the top shoots. Pruning is best carried out using sharp pruning shears.

GREEN THUMB GUIDE

Watering and feeding
Water generously during the active growth period, keeping the soil thoroughly moist. Do not allow the pot to stand in water. In winter, let the plant rest, watering just enough to prevent the soil from drying out. Feed with water-soluble fertilizer every two weeks during late spring and summer.

Light and temperature
Acalyphas need plenty of light. A position in a south- or west-facing window, with sunlight filtered through a sheer curtain, is ideal in summer; in winter, they need about four hours of direct sunshine daily. Warmth is essential if these plants are to flourish. Keep them in temperatures of up to 80°F, but not below 60°F.

Soil and repotting
Use a soil-based potting mix. If the plant is worth keeping once its roots have filled the existing pot, repot it to a pot one size larger. This should be done in spring, but the plant grows so vigorously it may need repotting more than once a year.

Given plenty of warmth and filtered sunshine,
Acalypha hispida bears fringelike plumes of tiny red
flowers.

Achimenes

ACHIMENES LONGIFLORA

Laden with masses of colorful blooms, *Achimenes longiflora*, a relative of the African violet, makes a vivid display in the flowering season. It comes from the warm, humid parts of Mexico, Central America and Jamaica and its common names include hot-water plant, Cupid's bower and magic flower. A member of the Gesneriaceae family, it has a host of related species and varieties. Some particularly attractive examples include *A. longiflora* '*Alba*', and the hybrids *A. l.* 'Ambroise Verschaffelt', 'Tarentella' and 'Fritz Michelssen'. These and other hybrids bear flowers in a rainbow of colors such as pale blue, pink, yellow, deep red and purple.

The foliage of *A. longiflora* is also attractive. Its distinctly sawtooth-edged leaves are up to $3\frac{1}{2}$ inches long and $1\frac{1}{2}$ inches wide, and generally dark-green in color. Its trailing stems, up to 2 feet long, make it an attractive plant for a hanging basket.

All forms of achimenes develop a root system from which grow a number of small rhizomes, measuring about 1 inch long and $\frac{1}{4}$ inch thick. Each rhizome sends up a single stem that carries pairs of heart-shaped leaves on short stalks.

The flowers borne on these short stalks are narrow and tubular, flaring out into five rounded lobes, which measure up to 2 inches long and 3 inches across. Although the individual blooms are short-lived, the flowering season extends from June through September.

Once the flowering season is over, the leaves of the plant shrivel. When they have dried out, cut off the stems just above the surface of the potting mix. Set the dormant plant in its container in a shady cool place until spring.

Achimenes can be propagated from seed, from cuttings, from young shoots or from newly sprouting rhizomes. Sow seeds in spring in moist, but not sodden, soil – if the soil is too wet the seeds will not germinate. Give more water once the plants have grown a mass of leaves. To speed up germination, provide bottom heat to the seeds.

To propagate from rhizomes, take those left dormant over the winter out of the old pot. Give them a good shake to remove excess soil and carefully separate them out. Some people say that the plant's common name of hot water plant comes from the belief that plunging the rhizomes into hot water before planting makes them develop leaves more quickly.

A. longiflora looks particularly attractive in a hanging basket. To create the best effect, plant at least a dozen rhizomes together and you will be rewarded with a glowing mass of color.

Plant containers can take the most unexpected forms. The vivid purple blooms and pretty foliage of *Achimenes longiflora* are displayed to good effect in this colorful cookie tin.

PROPAGATION

Achimenes is easy to propagate from its prolific underground rhizomes.
1 Remove the soil from pieces of rhizome and break them into $\frac{1}{2}$-inch lengths.
2 Plant rhizome pieces in fairly shallow pots. Place each about $\frac{1}{2}$ inch below the surface of fresh potting mix. Do not press the potting mix down too firmly, since this can cause waterlogging.
3 Water well and drain very thoroughly. Cover the pot with a clear plastic bag supported on a wire hoop. Tie the bag with string round the rim of the pot. Leave in a warm, light spot until leaves develop.

GREEN THUMB GUIDE

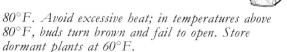

Watering and feeding

Water Achimenes with care, using tepid, soft water. After potting up, and until a good root system has developed, water sparingly. Once growth is well established, water generously, but allow the surface of the potting mix to dry out between waterings. As the flowering season nears its end, start to reduce watering.

Before the plants begin flowering, feed every two weeks with a nitrogen-rich water-soluble fertilizer. When the buds have formed, use fertilizer that contains more phosphate and potash than nitrogen.

Light and temperature

Actively growing plants need bright light but not direct sunshine. While dormant in winter they need little light, but will not tolerate frost. During the growing season, keep the plant at between 60°F and 80°F. Avoid excessive heat; in temperatures above 80°F, buds turn brown and fail to open. Store dormant plants at 60°F.

Soil and repotting

Use a mixture of equal parts of peat moss, coarse sand or perlite, and vermiculite. These plants do not like acid soil so, to reduce the level of acidity, add three or four teaspoonfuls of dolomite lime or crushed egg-shells to four cups of mixture. Repot newly sprouting rhizomes in spring as described opposite.

Urn plant
AECHMEA FASCIATA

The spectacular aechmeas grow in tropical mountainous regions of an area stretching from Mexico to Argentina. They are epiphytic bromeliads – they do not root themselves in the earth but grow on tree branches or rocks. Like all epiphytes, they use other plants only as supports; they take no nourishment from them. All have dramatic floral spikes and rosettes of leaves that form vaselike cups at their bases. The plants draw their nourishment from the rainwater and debris that collects in these cups.

The urn plant (*Aechmea fasciata*) from Brazil is one of the most popular aechmeas and the easiest to grow as a houseplant. Its gray-green, straplike leaves are armed with spines at their edges and banded with silver markings; they are about 2 feet in length.

When the urn plant reaches maturity, after three or four years of growth, it sends up a flowerhead bearing a conical rosette of pink bracts. These bracts are interspersed with small flowers that are blue at first but later turn to pinkish-red. Although the true flowers soon wither, the decorative pink bracts remain for about six months.

The urn plant flowers only once, but new plants can be grown from the side shoots which appear after flowering is over. Remove these with a sharp knife when they are about one-third of the size of the parent plant. Cut them as close as possible to the base and allow them to dry out for a few days before planting. Plant in lime-free soil and give some support until the roots are well established. It can then be moved into direct sun.

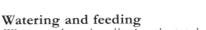

GREEN THUMB GUIDE

Watering and feeding
Water moderately, allowing the top half of the soil to dry out partially between waterings. Keep the central cup filled with fresh water, but do not allow the same water to remain there for too long or it will become stagnant and smelly. If possible, use rainwater and avoid the risk of lime deposits from hard water appearing on the leaves.

Feed with half-strength water-soluble fertilizer every two weeks. Apply the feed to the roots and to the central cup.

Light and temperature
Aechmeas need full sunlight to grow best. Without sun they will not flower successfully. Temperatures above 60°F are essential, although in winter the plants will tolerate a temperature down to, but not below, 50°F. Keep humidity high by misting daily.

Soil and repotting
Use a mixture of equal parts of leaf mold, peat moss and coarse sand or perlite. Repotting is not necessary. Instead, remove well-grown offsets and plant them up as described above.

MAKING A BROMELIAD LOG

Aechmeas grow perfectly well in pots, but for a more interesting display, grow them on a branch – as in the wild. Find a piece of tree branch, preferably with at least one fork, and set it in plaster-of-Paris and pebbles in a large container. Take the plant out of its pot and wrap moistened sphagnum moss around its roots. Bind the moss lightly with plastic-covered wire to keep it together.

Choose a position on the branch – aechmeas like to be in a fork or crevice, so, if necessary, scrape away a little bark to provide a suitable site. Attach the moss-covered base to the branch with more plastic-covered wire. Once some roots appear through the moss, remove the wire. Mist the plant and its roots daily to keep it moist and healthy and make sure its "vase" is topped up with rainwater.

At the center of its cluster of arching, gray-green, spiny leaves, the urn plant (*Aechmea fasciata*) develops a striking, conical rosette of pale-pink bracts. These bracts are interspersed with delicate flowers, which are pale blue when they first appear but turn to pinkish red.

Aechmea gigantea (*syn. Chevalieria sphaerocephala*) is similar to the urn plant in many respects, but has a stout, erect stalk which can grow to 2 feet long. Its leaves are a brighter green and its flower bracts are brilliant red.

Even after the urn plant's tiny flowers have faded, its spectacular pink bracts make an attractive display for up to six months.

Aeschynanthus

AESCHYNANTHUS

Members of the genus aeschynanthus are known as basket plants because they look their best in hanging baskets. All the hundred or so species of aeschynanthus have elegantly trailing stems, which are up to 3 feet long and tipped with tubular flowers. Like the ever-popular African violet, they belong to the Gesneriaceae family.

Aeschynanthus plants come from a large area stretching from the Himalayas to Borneo and New Guinea, where they thrive in the high humidity of the warm monsoon and rain forests. All are epiphytes – plants that have no roots in the soil but grow above ground level, supported by other plants. In the wild, aeschynanthus plants grow on trees, their woody stems trailing over the moss-covered branches.

Perhaps the most spectacular species is *A. speciosus*, with its glossy foliage and colorful flowers. The narrow, dark-green leaves are about 4 inches long and 1½ inches wide. At each stem tip, 4 to 8 of these leaves surround a cluster of 6 to 20 flowers which are yellow-orange, shading to glowing red. This species has stiffer branches than most aeschynanthus plants and can be grown in a pot without support.

A. pulcher, however, is one species that is best in a hanging basket. The paired leaves on its trailing stems are thick and edged with reddish-brown. Clusters of reddish-brown tubular cups on the upper parts of the stems each contain a red flower.

While the flowers of another popular houseplant species *A. marmoratus* are rather insignificant, its foliage is extremely attractive. The fleshy leaves are light-green above, marbled with darker markings, while the undersides are flushed with rich red. Each leaf is about 4 inches long and 1½ inches wide. The flowers are greenish-yellow, with a touch of brown at the throat.

The flower buds of *A. radicans* resemble red lipsticks, hence the plant's popular name of lipstick vine. Its glossy, pointed leaves are soft and gray when young, and scarlet flowers emerge from the "lipstick cases" at the tips of the stems between late spring and midsummer.

Aeschynanthus plants can be propagated by tip cuttings or by layering. Take cuttings, about 3 inches in length, in late spring from nonflowering shoots. Plant them in a mix of equal parts of peat and sand and keep at a temperature of 65°F to 70°F. The method for layering is described below.

To propagate by layering, bend a branch down and secure in a pot of moistened coarse sphagnum moss. Once some roots have formed, cut off the branch and allow the new plant to develop on its own.

GREEN THUMB GUIDE

Watering and feeding
Water aeschynanthus generously while in flower. At other times water moderately, just enough to keep the soil moist throughout. Feed monthly with a diluted water-soluble fertilizer. These jungle dwellers need high humidity so mist daily and, if possible, place trays of moist pebbles below the trailing stems.

Light and temperature
Bright filtered light is best for these plants, for about two to four hours daily. Keep them in an average room temperature, and never lower than 55°F.

Soil and repotting
Use a mix of equal parts of peat moss, perlite and vermiculite, or use coarse sphagnum moss on its own. Leave the potting mix lightly packed to allow essential aeration around the roots. Repot at any time of year, but only when the roots have filled the existing pot. Move the plant into a pot one size larger.

With its clusters of glowing, orange-red flowers, the
spectacular *Aeschynanthus speciosus* adds a welcome
splash of color to any room.

Grow *Aeschynanthus pulcher* in a hanging basket so that its trailing stems droop down, displaying their tubular, deep-red flowers.

Another attractive species, *Aeschynanthus hildebrandii*, has bright-red flowers with white pistils.

Golden trumpet

ALLAMANDA CATHARTICA

The golden trumpet, *Allamanda cathartica*, is a vigorous climber with brilliant yellow flowers and evergreen leaves. A native of northern Brazil and Guyana, it thrives in hot and humid rain forests, where it climbs up the trunks of towering trees. It is a member of the Apocynaceae family.

Grown as a houseplant, the golden trumpet can reach a height of 10 or more feet. Support the plant with stakes or train its rambling growth onto a small trellis. With careful pruning, however, the plant can be made more bushy in shape and less tall. To make a bushy plant, cut it back by two-thirds in winter.

The glossy, dark-green leaves of allamanda are arranged in groups of three, and measure 4 to 6 inches long and $1\frac{1}{2}$ to $2\frac{1}{2}$ inches wide. The golden-yellow flowers are trumpet-shaped, flaring into five petals that span about 5 inches. Despite their beauty, these flowers are poisonous so should be kept well out of reach of children. Other popular hybrids include *A. c.* 'Grandiflora', a more compact plant with pale yellow flowers, and *A. c.* 'Hendersonii' which has reddish buds that eventually turn yellow.

Since these plants thrive in warm, humid conditions, they make a perfect choice for display in a plant window. A plant window is simply a double window, with space between the panes of glass large enough to accommodate plants. Plants with a fairly slender growth habit are best, and climbing varieties are ideal. This construction provides warmth and humidity for the plants and a more sophisticated form could even incorporate an automatic misting device, temperature control and lighting.

Otherwise, simply keep the plant in a light warm, spot – sunrooms and greenhouses are both suitable.

Propagate the golden trumpet by tip cuttings taken in spring or early summer. Take each cutting from below a node – a point where a leaf grows or grew. Dip the cut end in hormone rooting powder to encourage root growth. Fill a 3-inch pot with a mixture of peat moss and coarse sand, plant the cuttings and cover the whole pot with a clear plastic bag. Set the pot in a bright filtered light at a temperature of about 70°F. Once it has taken root, remove the plastic and treat it as a mature plant.

GREEN THUMB GUIDE

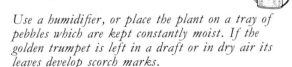

Watering and feeding

Water moderately throughout the active growth period of the plant, giving more if the weather becomes particularly warm. Water sparingly in winter while the plant is resting. Never leave the plant sitting in water.

Feed growing plants every two weeks from May through September, using a standard water-soluble fertilizer. In winter, give the resting plant a half-strength dose of fertilizer once a month.

Light and temperature

The golden trumpet must have plenty of sun and light, so does well in a warm, south-facing window or sunroom. Give the plant some protection from the sun's rays during the hottest part of the day. In winter, the plant needs at least four hours of direct light daily. If it does not have enough light, it will not bloom.

This is a demanding plant in terms of its need for warmth and humidity but, given the right conditions, it will bloom from June through September and more than reward your efforts. It must have a temperature of no less than 60°F throughout the year and will do well in much higher temperatures. Humidity must also be kept high.

Use a humidifier, or place the plant on a tray of pebbles which are kept constantly moist. If the golden trumpet is left in a draft or in dry air its leaves develop scorch marks.

In winter the plant does tend to lose some leaves and look somewhat bald as a result. Don't worry – new, vigorous growth will appear in spring.

Soil and repotting

Use a standard potting mix containing equal parts of sterilized loam soil, peat moss, and coarse sand or perlite.

Repot in early spring if plants have outgrown their existing containers.

The golden trumpet (*Allamanda cathartica*) bears
brilliant yellow flowers throughout the summer.
(Warning! The flowers are poisonous.)

Flamingo flower

ANTHURIUM SCHERZERANUM

Brilliant red, glossy spathes make the flamingo flower (*Anthurium scherzeranum*) one of the most striking of flowering houseplants. A member of the Araceae family, it comes from tropical areas of Central and South America.

The leathery, dark-green leaves of *A. scherzeranum* are up to 8 inches long and 3 inches wide, and borne on leafstalks also measuring up to 8 inches. But the main attractions of the plant are its large, glossy, brilliant red bracts, or spathes, each pierced by a twisting orange spadix – a fleshy spike bearing tiny flowers. The spadix is 2 or 3 inches long. Some varieties have darker red spathes, spotted with white.

Other attractive anthuriums include *A. andraeanum*, also known as the oilcloth flower or flamingo lily, which has deep-green, heart-shaped leaves and red or white flower spathes. Unfortunately this species is difficult to grow indoors. The crystal anthurium or strap flower (*A. crystallinum*) is primarily cultivated for its highly decorative foliage. Its leaves, which can be up to 2 feet long and 1 foot wide, are metallic blue when young, turning to deep emerald-green as they age.

Although the plants normally flower in summer, in ideal conditions they may bloom on and off throughout most of the year. Anthuriums do best in bright, filtered light with temperatures of at least 60°F. Display the plant on its own to show off its unusual flower structure. A simple container will not distract from the dramatic beauty of the plant.

To propagate the flamingo flower, divide overcrowded clumps in spring. Separate them carefully so that each section includes some roots and a growing point. Shake off excess soil and plant each section in its own pot containing a fresh peat-based potting mix. Place the pot in a position where it receives medium light and maintain a temperature of about 70°F. Keep the mixture moist and the atmosphere humid until growth is established.

An electrically heated propagator with a thermostat to maintain a constant temperature makes it much easier to propagate these plants successfully. *A. crystallinum* can also be grown from seed sown in a heated propagating case.

GREEN THUMB GUIDE

Watering and feeding
Water plentifully during the active growing period. Do not overwater, however, since this may rot the plant's roots. In winter, while the plant is resting, allow the top half-inch of soil to dry out between waterings. If possible, use lime-free water or rainwater.

Feed with half-strength water-soluble fertilizer every two weeks while the plant is growing.

Light and temperature
Do not expose plants to direct sunlight. They do best in bright, filtered light and can be kept in a partially shaded window throughout the year. Too little light will make the leaves elongated and unattractive.

These plants come from humid tropical rain forests. Accordingly, they are happiest in temperatures between 65°F and 70°F, but will tolerate a low of 55°F for brief periods. High humidity is essential if they are to flower well, so mist frequently and stand the pots on trays of damp pebbles. Wipe the leaves regularly to free them of any dust.

Soil and repotting
Use a potting mix containing equal parts of fir bark and coarse sphagnum moss. To ensure adequate drainage, place pieces of clay pot in the bottom of the pot to a depth of about 2 inches.

Repot new plants into pots one size larger in spring. Subsequently, repot only every third year.

Tall flower stalks may need some form of support to keep them from drooping. Push thin canes into the soil around the sides of the pot and tie the flower stalks to them with plastic-covered wire or twine.

The Flamingo flower (*Anthurium scherzeranum*) bears
shiny red spathes, pierced by tiny floral spikes. These
exotic blooms are long-lasting and, in ideal
conditions, the plant will flower for much of the year.

19

Begonia

BEGONIA

The genus *Begonia* (Begoniaceae family) includes more than 1,000 species and 10,000 hybrids and cultivars from all over the world, many of them popular as houseplants. The begonia was named after an eighteenth-century French botanist, M. Michel Begon. The many varieties are prized for their colorful flowers, decorative foliage or a combination of both.

Begonias can be divided into three groups, depending on the type of root structure or storage organs they have; the three types are fibrous-rooted, tuberous and rhizomatous.

Plants of the first type, fibrous-rooted, have a root system similar to that of most other plants. Tuberous begonias have underground tubers with juicy stems that have a storage organ at their base. These plants undergo a period of dormancy when the top growth dies down. During this time they need virtually no water. Rhizomatous begonias have rhizomes that creep over the surface of the potting mix sending down roots. They store some water and plant food in the rhizomes, so can tolerate periods of neglect.

Of the fibrous-rooted group of begonias, *B.* × *semperflorens-cultorum* is probably the most popular. It is often grown outdoors and is also known as the wax or bedding begonia. Its name *"semperflorens"* means ever-blooming – an apt description for this plant which can flower for most of the year. A bushy plant, it has fleshy stems, 6 to 15 inches tall, and bears waxy, dark-green to bronze-red leaves. There are many hybrids, with flowers in white, pink, red or bicolors. Some worthy of note are *B. s.* 'Dainty Maid', which has white flowers with the outer petals tipped with pink; *B. s.* 'Fiesta' which has scarlet, single-layered flowers with prominent yellow stamens; and *B.s.* 'Gustav Lind' with many-petaled pink flowers.

One very popular begonia is the Christmas-flowering begonia (*B.* × *cheimantha*) which blooms profusely in winter. Its medium-green stems are up to 18 inches tall and it has glossy green leaves and solitary pink flowers. After flowering it becomes semidormant until spring.

An attractive tuberous plant is *B.* × *hiemalis* including two hybrids, *B. h.* 'Fireglow' and *B. h.* 'Schwabenland', that have glossy, deep-green leaves and bright-red flowers with prominent yellow centers.

B. limmingheiana (syn. *B. glaucophylla*) is a rhizo-

GREEN THUMB GUIDE

Watering and feeding

Water all types of begonias moderately during the active growth period, allowing the top inch of the potting mix to dry out between waterings. In winter, for the fibrous-rooted and rhizomatous begonias, allow the top half of the soil to dry out before watering again. For tuberous begonias, reduce watering as the growth dies down. For those plants that lose their stems and foliage in winter, stop watering once the leaves turn yellow.

Feed fibrous-rooted and rhizomatous begonias every two weeks while actively growing, using a standard water-soluble fertilizer. Feed tuberous begonias with a fertilizer high in potash every two weeks during the active growth period.

Light and temperature

Fibrous-rooted and rhizomatous begonias which are cultivated mainly for their foliage need bright light, but not direct sun. Flowering varieties need three to four hours of direct sunshine daily. All tuberous begonias need bright, filtered light throughout the year.

Normal room temperatures suit begonias. In the winter rest period, maintain a temperature of about 60°F; dormant plants should be kept cooler at about 55°F. To increase humidity around the plants, set pots on trays of moist pebbles.

Soil and repotting

For all groups, use either a peat-based potting mix or blend equal parts of standard soil-based potting mix and peat moss.

Repot fibrous-rooted plants every spring into pots one size larger.

Rhizomatous begonias have shallow roots and are best planted in half-pots or shallow containers. Only repot when the rhizomes have spread across the entire surface of the potting mix.

Plant tubers of B. × tuberhybrida *in trays of moistened peat moss so that they are half in and half out of the soil; the concave side of the tuber should be uppermost. Once some top growth appears, move the plants to 4-inch pots containing the recommended potting mix. The smaller tubers of other tuberous begonias can be planted directly into 4-inch pots.*

matous begonia that comes from Brazil. In the wild it creeps over the ground, putting down roots from its nodes wherever it comes into contact with a suitable soil, or climbs up moss-covered tree trunks. Its shiny, oval leaves are medium-green in color, and up to 5 inches long and 3 inches wide. A winter-flowering plant, it produces attractive brick-red blooms.

Begonia plants can be raised from seed or propagated in the way suitable for their type. Multiply fibrous-rooted begonias by tip cuttings. Take the cuttings in spring and dip the cut end of each stem in hormone rooting powder. Plant in a moistened mixture of equal parts of peat moss and coarse sand. Cover the pot with a plastic bag and leave until some growth indicates that the cuttings have rooted. Do not overwater or they may rot. After six months, move the plants to larger pots of standard soil mix and treat as mature begonias.

Rhizomatous begonias can be propagated in the same way but, with the exception of *B. limmingheiana*, can also be propagated by leaf cuttings. In spring, take a leaf with 1 to 2 inches of leafstalk. Make small cuts in the leaf where the main veins intersect and plant it in rooting mix in such a way that it rests on the soil. Enclose the pot in a clear plastic bag. About six weeks later, plantlets should have appeared from the leaf. Plant these singly in 3-inch pots filled with a standard potting mix.

Propagate tuberous begonias from bulbils – small tubers that form in the leaf axils. In fall, remove these bulbils and store them in a dry place at a temperature of about 55°F. In spring, plant the bulbils in a seed tray. Once they have grown about $2\frac{1}{2}$ inches high, plant them in individual pots and treat them as mature plants. They will not, however, flower profusely until their second year.

The winter-flowering *Begonia × hiemalis* 'Nixe' produces a mass of semi-double deep-pink blooms.

Begonia × cheimantha is grown to produce its pretty pink, single-layered flowers in time for the winter holiday season. This is an extremely popular variety but, since it does not often bloom a second year, it is usually discarded after flowering.

A variety of *Begonia × cheimantha* bears a host of white, single-layered flowers. Displayed in an attractive container, this plant can look most impressive and makes a particularly pretty table decoration.

Begonia × hiemalis 'Anita' is a charming bushy plant with single-layered, red flowers adorned with prominent yellow centers. It blooms in fall.

The handsome *Begonia × hiemalis* 'Schwabenland' has
glowing red flowers, perfectly set off by glossy, dark-
green leaves.

A creamy-yellow variety of *Begonia × hiemalis* 'Schwabenland' is attractively displayed in wicker baskets.

TUBER PROPAGATION

Begonia tubers produce growth buds where new plants will start.

To propagate tuberous begonias, lift the tubers in spring. Shake off excess potting mix, then cut the tuber into two or three pieces. Make sure each piece bears a growing point.

Dust the sections with sulfur dust to prevent rotting. Plant sections $\frac{1}{2}$ inch deep, making sure the growing point is vertical and facing upwards.

The Brazilian *Begonia × semperflorens-cultorum* has glossy, almost waxy, dark-green leaves. It blooms profusely, bearing flowers with a mass of yellow stamens at their centers. Popular as a bedding plant for outdoor flower beds as well as for indoor display, it blooms at least from early summer through fall.

The beautiful *Begonia* × *hiemalis* 'Aphrodite' bears
stunning pink double flowers. This winter-flowering
variety is named for the goddess of love

Shrimp plant

BELOPERONE GUTTATA

In its native Mexico, the shrimp plant is a bushy, evergreen shrub that grows to about 3 feet high. As a houseplant, it is easy to cultivate and is tolerant of the warm, dry atmosphere of many modern homes. A synonym is *Justicia brandegeana*.

Grown indoors, this compact, vigorous plant reaches about 18 inches in height. Its leaves are soft, green and slightly hairy, but its salmon-pink petal-like floral bracts are its most striking feature. The overlapping structure of these bracts, and their color, resembles the body of a shrimp, hence the plant's popular name. In one variety of shrimp plant the bracts are bronze in color and another, 'Yellow Queen', has been developed with glowing yellow bracts.

The attractive bracts remain on the plant throughout summer and fall. The small, red-spotted white flowers that appear between them are, however, inconspicuous and short-lived.

When buying a shrimp plant, choose one that is young, with a compact bushy shape. Avoid plants with long, straggly stems. If the bracts are to keep their color the plant must have good natural light. Place it by a window in strong light – it will enjoy some direct sunlight.

Once positioned, the shrimp plant is easy to care for, needing little attention other than regular watering and feeding and annual pruning and repotting. Pinch out dead flowers and remove any bracts that are losing their color.

Brown or black patches on the leaves of a shrimp plant can be a sign of overwatering. If these occur, reduce the amount of water you give slightly – this should clear up the problem. Leaves with mottled or yellow patches warn of infestation by red spider mite and you may need to spray with insecticide to destroy the pests. Red spider mites thrive in a hot dry atmosphere so, once the plant has been treated, move it somewhere cooler and mist the leaves regularly to help prevent further attacks.

After the flowering period, the shrimp plant needs a short winter rest at a lower-than-normal temperature. Move it to a position in good, but not bright, natural light, in a maximum temperature of about 55°F to 60°F. It may shed a few leaves during this period.

In early spring, repot the plant, using fresh, loam-based potting mix. After repotting, prune to maintain the plant's compact shape. Cut back all the branches, and, with a young plant, pinch out growing tips to promote bushy growth and lush foliage. Remove some of the young plant's first flowers, too, to encourage growth.

Propagate shrimp plants by tip cuttings. When pruning in spring, take cuttings 2 to 3 inches long. Plant them in a small pot filled with soilless cutting mix, and cover the pot with a clear plastic bag to keep humidity high.

The cuttings should root easily and, once established, can be repotted into progressively larger pots. Alternatively, cuttings can be rooted in a propagator heated to around 65°F. As the cuttings grow, remove their growing tips and the first few flower bracts to give bushy, well-shaped plants.

GREEN THUMB GUIDE

Watering and feeding
Water freely with lime-free water during the growing period, keeping the soil constantly damp. In winter, water just enough to keep the potting mix from drying out. Start to increase watering after repotting in spring. Although the shrimp plant can tolerate a dry atmosphere, it will grow better with increased humidity. Stand the pot in a dish of damp pebbles and mist regularly. Feed with water-soluble fertilizer every two weeks throughout the growing season.

Light and temperature
In summer, place the plant in bright light, with some direct sun, to maintain the color of the bracts. In winter, leave it to rest in a shadier position. Normal room temperatures in centrally heated homes suit the shrimp plant well, but it likes cooler temperatures of about 55°F to 60°F in winter. Even in winter, the temperature should not drop below 45°F. Avoid sudden changes or extremes of temperature.

Soil
Use loam-based potting mix. Repot in spring, using a fresh mix.

Its striking pink bracts rather than its true flowers are
the attraction of the shrimp plant, *Beloperone guttata*.

Bougainvillea
BOUGAINVILLEA

This lush, shrubby climbing plant from Brazil, is also often seen in tropical and Mediterranean countries, where it creates a blaze of color over walls and balconies in the summer. The plant is named after its discoverer, the eighteenth-century French explorer and admiral Louis de Bougainville.

A few of the less vigorously climbing varieties of bougainvillea have been developed as houseplants. Their mid- or dark-green leaves are long and narrow and their stems woody; one variety, though, *B. spectabililis* has spiny stems. The white flowers are small and inconspicuous, but the surrounding papery bracts are brilliantly colored, creating the splendid display for which bougainvilleas are famed.

The most common species, *B. glabra*, has bracts of glowing magenta, and this is the color most commonly associated with the plant. Other varieties include 'Kiltie Campbell', with coppery red bracts that fade to magenta; the hybrid 'Poulton's Special', with bronze leaves and large purple bracts; and 'Mrs. Mclean', which has golden-yellow bracts fading to apricot and pink. The most popular variety is 'Mrs. Butt' (*B. × buttiana*) which has large rose-crimson bracts.

Bougainvillea bracts usually measure about 1 inch across and have a papery texture – in fact the plant is sometimes known as the paper flower.

Although rewarding, the bougainvillea is not the easiest houseplant to grow. It needs plenty of space, warmth and, above all, bright light, with about four hours of sunshine every day if it is to flower well. A sunroom or greenhouse is thus an ideal spot for a bougainvillea, or it can even be kept on a balcony or in a sunny part of the garden.

If kept outside, bougainvillea must be brought indoors before the first frosts. In an ideal position, with all its needs met, the bougainvillea grows 6 to 8 feet tall, but can be pruned to keep it to a more manageable height.

An established bougainvillea plant should be in a pot with a diameter of at least 8 inches to allow room for its roots. Train its climbing stems over wires or canes or let them cascade from a hanging basket. Keep the bougainvillea well watered and fed in the growing season and mist with lime-free water, particularly during hot weather or if the plant is in a hot room.

Red spider mite may infest bougainvillea. Mist plants thoroughly to discourage these pests, or use a commercial insecticide to destroy any mites. Aphids and mealy bugs may also attack the plant and need treating.

Leaves normally fall from the plant in winter, but leaves that turn yellow between the veins and remain on the plant are a sign of chlorosis. This is a problem caused by iron and manganese deficiency,

---

GREEN THUMB GUIDE

Watering and feeding
Always water and mist bougainvilleas with lime-free water. Lime in the water can cause a nutrient deficiency problem, resulting in discolored leaves.

Keep the plant well watered in the growing season. Decrease watering as the flowers begin to fade, and through the winter give just enough to keep the soil from drying out. When the plant starts to grow again in spring, increase the watering. Feed with diluted water-soluble fertilizer every two weeks during the growing season, but not at other times of year.

Light and temperature
Whether kept on a windowsill, in a sunroom or on an outside balcony, the bougainvillea must have bright light and plenty of sun if it is to reach its full flowering potential and produce richly-colored bracts. Four hours of sunshine a day is the ideal. During the summer growing season, keep the

bougainvillea at a temperature of 60°F to 70°F. In the winter rest period, a slightly lower temperature is best, but never below 45°F to 50°F.

Soil and repotting
Use a standard peat- or soil-based potting mix for a full-grown plant. Pot cuttings in three parts of potting mix to one part of coarse sand or perlite. Repot fast-growing young plants in spring when new shoots appear. Repot older, mature plants only when really necessary.

itself brought about by the lime in water. Treat an affected plant with Sequestrene (chelated iron) and be sure to use lime-free water for watering and misting.

Young, fast-growing plants should be repotted in spring when new shoots appear. Older, established plants should be repotted only when this is absolutely necessary, again in spring. Treat the roots with great care, disturbing them as little as possible.

Prune bougainvilleas immediately after flowering and again in early spring if you wish to restrict their size. Cut back main growth by a third and prune side shoots to two or three buds. Do not overprune new shoots since these bear the flowers.

Although bougainvilleas can be propagated from stem cuttings this is not an easy process. Take half-ripe stem cuttings in summer and, for the best chance of success, root them in a propagator with gentle bottom heat.

Given plenty of light and sun, the bougainvillea flowers profusely. Each small white bloom is surrounded by three gloriously colored bracts.

Variegated leaves distinguish this cultivar of
Bougainvillea glabra from other varieties. This specimen
has been trained over wire in an attractive shape.

A sunny windowsill is the best indoor site for a bougainvillea. Here, a well-grown plant will flower profusely throughout the summer. The plant may need the stronger light in a greenhouse or sunroom through the winter rest period, however, if it is to flower again the following year.

Depending on the variety, the spectacular bracts that are the bougainvillea's main attraction may be magenta, purple, red or even golden-yellow.

Bush violet

BROWALLIA SPECIOSA

Popularly known as the bush violet, the attractive *Browallia speciosa* flowers profusely in summer or winter, depending on when it was seeded. A plant started in fall, for example, blooms in winter. A South American plant, browallia is a member of the Solanaceae family and related to plants as diverse as petunias, potatoes and tomatoes. It is named after Bishop Browallius, close friend and biographer of the Swedish founder of modern botany, Carl Linnaeus.

The foliage of browallia is also pretty. Its drooping, glossy leaves are about 2 inches long and flowers are borne on frail, branching stems. The star-shaped, tubular flowers of *B. speciosa* are violet-blue with white throats and measure up to 2 inches across. Among the many hybrids are 'Major', with large blue flowers, 'Alba', with white flowers, and 'Sapphire', which is smaller than most browallias, reaching a height of only 6 to 8 inches. As blooms die, new ones appear and continue to do so for several months.

Although *B. speciosa* can reach a height of about 24 inches, it is best kept to a more manageable 14 inches or so. Pinch out the growing tips to keep the plant an attractive bushy shape.

Buy the plant when in flower and place it in a cool airy room, shaded from direct sun. Browallia will not flower well in a hot, dry atmosphere and needs plenty of cool air around it. Given the right conditions, browallia is easy to care for. Mist the leaves occasionally and pick off the flowers as they fade – new ones will bloom in their place. The plant may need staking to prevent it sprawling.

Do not bother to repot your browallia for a second season. These are annual plants and rarely bloom well a second year. Old plants become thin and ugly. Take cuttings after flowering and discard the old plant.

Browallias can be grown from seeds or cuttings. Seeds are easier to grow, but plants grown from cuttings produce the best flowers.

Sow seeds in early spring for summer flowers, in summer or fall for winter flowering. Sow in pots, just below the soil surface, and cover the pots with clear plastic bags to increase humidity. Keep the pots in a warm place to encourage germination. Once some growth appears, remove the plastic bags. Transfer the sturdiest seedlings to 3-inch pots, three to a pot. Replant in 5-inch pots when the roots fill the containers. When the seedlings are 4 inches high, remove their tops – these can be planted as cuttings.

Plant cuttings, from old or new plants, in 5-inch pots and keep them warm and moist. Once growth is established, treat them as mature plants.

For a particularly striking display of these plants, put several different varieties together in a tub, or place two or three pots in one container.

In contrast to the brilliant blues and purples of many browallia species, the hybrid 'Alba' bears delicate, white flowers.

GREEN THUMB GUIDE

Watering and feeding
Water sparingly in fall and winter, just enough to keep the potting mix damp. In spring and summer, water more freely so that the mix is evenly damp throughout. Never allow the plant to dry out, but do make sure that it has good drainage – the soil should not become waterlogged. Mist occasionally, particularly if the atmosphere becomes at all dry. This plant cannot tolerate dry air and should never be kept in a centrally-heated room, unless you have a humidifier.

Feed every two weeks during the growing period, with diluted water-soluble fertilizer.

Light and temperature
Browallia cannot tolerate extremes of temperature. Keep the plant in a cool room at a temperature of about 55°F; do not let the temperature fall below 50°F. It must have bright light – browallia will not produce flowers if in a poor light. Some sunshine is needed if it is to bloom prolifically, but sunlight should be filtered, not falling directly on the plant.

Soil
For cuttings and mature seedlings, use equal parts of peat moss or leaf mold and potting mix. Sow seeds in a light mix.

Take off excess top-growth to keep your browallia in an attractive compact shape. Group two or three such plants in a container for an eye-catching display.

Chameleon plant

BRUNFELSIA PAUCIFLORA

Sweet-scented flowers bloom almost year round on this slow-growing, evergreen plant from Brazil. Commonly cultivated as an outdoor shrub in warmer climates, *Brunfelsia pauciflora* can also be grown as a houseplant and reaches about 2 feet in height. It is a member of the Solanaceae family.

The foliage of *B. pauciflora* is glossy, dark-green; each pointed leathery leaf reaches a length of about 3 inches. The fragrant flower is made up of a long tube that opens out into five flat petals; the whole bloom is about 2 inches across. The color of newly opened flowers is violet-purple but changes to pinkish-blue and then finally to white – a sequence that gave rise to the plant's common names of chameleon plant and yesterday, today and tomorrow. In ideal conditions brunfelsia blooms almost continually, resting only for a few weeks in late winter or spring.

A related plant, *B. undulata*, which comes from the West Indies, bears creamy white flowers and

The fragrant flowers of *Brunfelsia pauciflora* are violet-blue when they first appear, but gradually turn pinkish-blue, then white.

grows up to 4 feet indoors with a spread of 2 feet.

To get the best blooms from your plant, keep it at a constant, moderate temperature and away from drafts. Mist regularly, particularly in summer, to keep the atmosphere around it humid – air that is too dry and hot discourages flowering and attracts aphids. Brunfelsia needs plenty of bright light but cannot tolerate too much direct sunshine. Strong sun should be filtered through a sheer curtain.

Yellowing leaves can be a sign of chlorosis, a deficiency of iron and manganese caused by lime in the plant's soil or water. Feed the plant with a fertilizer containing these elements and always use lime-free water for misting and watering. To ensure water is lime-free, use rainwater or tap water that has been boiled and left to stand for 24 hours.

When the plant stops flowering in late winter or spring, let it rest for a few weeks at about 55°F– 50°F is the absolute minimum. This rest period is essential if the plant is to develop new flower buds. Water just enough to keep the soil damp and do not feed during this time. Take the chance to prune any ragged, untidy stems to keep the plant compact. Once the plant is growing actively again, pinch out growing tips to encourage bushiness and the formation of new flower buds.

To propagate B. calycina, take stem cuttings of half-ripe shoots in spring or early summer. Plant several in a 3-inch pot containing a mix of equal parts of peat and coarse sand. Given a temperature of about 70°F, the cuttings should root in about four weeks.

DOUBLE POTTING

A neat way to prevent a brunfelsia being adversely affected by low humidity is to double pot it. Set the plant in an unglazed terracotta pot. Place this pot in a wide, outer pot filled with damp peat. Water the peat regularly – enough to keep it constantly damp but not soggy. This method will also keep the potting soil evenly moist. Just be sure not to overwater.

GREEN THUMB GUIDE

Watering and feeding
From spring through fall water B. pauciflora *regularly, keeping the soil evenly moist. Mist frequently with tepid water. Always use lime-free water for misting and watering – lime causes mineral deficiencies which turn the plant's leaves yellow. In winter, keep the plant only just damp but never let it dry out completely.*

Feed every week from April through September with diluted water-soluble fertilizer.

Light and temperature
Keep the plant in bright light throughout the summer. Make sure, however, that it is shaded from the direct glare and heat of the sun – a south-facing window is not suitable. In winter, it needs full daylight and will appreciate occasional exposure to the weaker rays of winter sun.

Cool to average temperatures suit B. pauciflora *best – it will not flower in high temperatures. In*

summer, 62°F to 68°F is ideal; in winter, it needs lower temperatures of 50°F to 58°F. It cannot tolerate temperatures below these and must also be protected from sudden fluctuations in temperature.

Soil and repotting
Use a good peat-based mix or one rich in humus. Repot B. pauciflora *only when really necessary, using a lime-free soil mix that allows good drainage.*

Calathea
CALATHEA CROCATA

There are over 150 varieties of calathea, many of them prized as houseplants for their strikingly patterned and colorful foliage. Calatheas come from the humid jungles of Brazil and, when grown indoors, thrive in the steamy conditions of domestic bathrooms and greenhouses.

One species of calathea is rather different from its relatives, and far less commonly grown. An ideal plant for the enthusiast in search of something different, *Calathea crocata* is one of very few calatheas, and the only houseplant variety that produces flowers.

C. crocata blooms in spring. Tall slender stems bear deep-golden-yellow bracts that form globular flowerheads, some 2 inches across. When in flower, the plant reaches a height of about 15 inches. Flowering lasts for several weeks, and the plant may bloom a second time in the same year. To increase the likelihood of a second flowering, keep the plant at a steady temperature, between 65°F and 70°F, and let it have no more than 10 hours of light each day.

Although most calatheas have highly decorative foliage, *C. crocata* has plain leaves that are narrow, dark green and up to 7 inches long. They do, however, provide an admirable foil for the plant's golden crown of flowers.

Like many unusual houseplants, *C. crocata* is not always easy to grow. It cannot tolerate a hot, dry atmosphere and will flower only in average warmth with high humidity. If summer weather does become too dry for this native of the jungle, try giving it its own high-humidity environment. Place a saucer upside down in a deep bowl, wide enough to take the plant's pot. Pour in water to just below the high point of the saucer and stand the plant on the saucer. The water does not actually touch the pot but keeps the air around the plant comfortably moist.

Unlike the foliage calatheas, *C. crocata* thrives in bright light and does well in a garden room or at an east- or west-facing window, provided it is shaded from direct sun. In winter keep the plant in a well-lit, but sunless, position with a minimum temperature of 55°F. With luck, it should survive to flower another year.

C. crocata can be hard to obtain. It is seldom seen in stores, but a specialist grower should be able to provide a good specimen. Once you have a plant, propagate it by division. In spring, divide the most overcrowded clumps, making sure that some roots remain in each section. Plant each part in a 3-inch pot filled with a mix of three parts of standard potting mix to one part of peat. Cover the pot with a clear plastic bag to keep humidity high and place in average warmth and light. Once some new growth is established, remove the plastic bag.

C. crocata does best in shallow pots. If you have only deep pots available, half-fill one with broken crocks before adding any soil.

GREEN THUMB GUIDE

Watering and feeding
Keep the soil of C. crocata *evenly moist. In winter give less water; if the soil is too damp in winter the roots are liable to rot. Always use lime-free water for watering and misting.*

Keep the plant in a humid atmosphere. Place its pot in a larger container of damp peat and mist the leaves regularly to keep the air around them damp. If the weather becomes very hot and dry, try placing the plant on a saucer in a bowl of water as described above.

Feed with liquid fertilizer every week from April through August.

Light and temperature
Unlike other calathea plants whose leaves lose their glory when exposed to strong light, C. crocata *grows well and flowers its best in a well-lit position. Do not, however, leave it in direct sunshine. In winter, keep it in a completely sunless position.*

Summer temperatures of 65°F to 70°F are ideal for C. crocata. *Winter temperatures can be slightly lower but should not fall below 55°F. Sudden changes in temperature can be harmful.*

Soil and repotting
Use a light, porous, peaty soil which is well aerated, both for repotting and for planting divided sections from old plants.

The only houseplant variety of calathea to flower,
C. crocata bears deep-yellow blooms on long slender
stems.

Slipper flower

CALCEOLARIA HYBRIDA

Although this South American plant blooms only for a month or so in spring or summer, its vivid, pouchlike flowers make it well worth a place in your home during its brief period of glory. There are many calceolaria hybrids available, which bear brilliant yellow, orange, red, pink or bronze flowers, often with brown or purple markings.

The two-lipped flowers cluster at the top of the plant on long stalks. The upper lip of each is small but the lower is bulbous and has a shape that has inspired many common names, including slipper flower, lady's slipper, lady's pocketbook, pouch flower and slipperwort. Each flower measures 1 to 2 inches across. The plant's leaves are up to 6 inches across and covered with soft hairs. Many slipper flowers grow to about 18 inches tall, but the popular dwarf strains, such as 'Multiflora Nana,' are only 8 to 10 inches tall.

Calceolaria, a member of the Scrophulariaceae family, is an annual that is best grown from seed. Sow seeds from February onward, or buy a plant in spring or summer when it is just about to flower. Choose a specimen with plenty of flower buds and with healthy leaves that are not marked or damaged.

If your plant is to bloom profusely it needs a situation that is cool, bright and well-ventilated, but away from both direct sun and drafts. An east- or west-facing window is often suitable. Slipper flowers will not thrive in a dry, over-heated room.

Moderate temperatures, humid air and regular watering and feeding all help to prolong a calceolaria's flowering period and encourage an abundance of its colorful blooms. Moreover, these conditions also discourage aphids, which are attracted to calceolaria, particularly if the atmosphere around the plant is hot and dry. The aphids congregate on the growing tips and buds, and should be treated immediately with the appropriate pesticide before they do too much damage.

Do not repot a calceolaria once flowering is finished; it will not bloom a second year and must be discarded. If, however, you buy a small plant or a plant that is in a small pot, repot it into a 5- or 6-inch pot. A few weeks later, when the plant is growing vigorously, repot it again into an 8- or 9-inch pot.

Calceolaria plants are notoriously difficult to propagate. Since they are easily available from garden centers and florists, it makes sense to purchase fully grown plants about to burst into flower rather than struggling to grow them from seed. If you do wish to try, sow seeds in spring or summer, and keep the growing plants in a cool greenhouse at a temperature of about 55°F until the following year's flowering period.

To create a particularly bright display with these unusual plants, place several varieties, with different flower colors, in a hanging basket, or group calceolarias with other flowering plants.

GREEN THUMB GUIDE

Watering and feeding
Water calceolarias regularly, but only just enough to keep the potting mix barely moist; it should never become soggy. Make sure when watering that no water falls onto the leaves or flowers. Any drops will mark the leaves and also encourage the development of fungal diseases.

The plants need moist air but cannot be misted since the water would damage the leaves. Instead, keep them in a humid place, such as a bathroom, or set a pot or group of pots on a dish of pebbles, which are kept moist. Alternatively, place pots in larger containers full of damp peat.

Encourage profuse flowering by feeding plants with dilute water-soluble fertilizer. Once in bloom, however, plants should not be fed.

Light and temperature
Keep slipper flowers in a brightly lit position but shaded from the heat and glare of direct sunshine. Cool temperatures suit them best — they thrive at between 50°F and 55°F. Do not expose them to temperatures above 60°F.

Soil and repotting
To repot a small plant or one bought in a small pot, use a potting mix that allows good drainage.

If attempting to raise plants from seed, use a fresh, fine soil mix. Dampen the soil before sowing the seeds.

The curious pouchlike flowers of calceolaria make a
brilliant show for several weeks in spring or summer.
There are many species and varieties, with blooms
varying in color from vibrant yellow to orange, red
or bronze.

Camellia

CAMELLIA JAPONICA

Camellias are renowned for their exquisite white, pink or red blooms and handsome, glossy foliage. There are about 82 species of these evergreen trees and shrubs, many of which can be grown as houseplants. Camellias belong to the Theaceae family.

A native of south Asia, the camellia grows in mountainous woodland, reaching a height of 50 feet or more. Its original name, *Thea japonica*, is obsolete and it is now universally known as camellia after the missionary George Joseph Kamel who first brought a specimen to Europe in the seventeenth century. In the nineteenth century the camellia became popular as a cultivated plant, and in Europe and North America was grown in elegant conservatories and verandas, and also as a houseplant.

The camellia is an evergreen. Its serrated oval leaves are dark-green and glossy and a perfect foil for the roselike flowers. Most varieties of *C. japonica* grow to about 2 feet in three years; other varieties grown as houseplants, such as *C. reticulata* and *C. sasanqua*, may grow somewhat faster and need to be pruned back to keep their height manageable.

Depending on the variety, the camellia's blooms may be single, semidouble or double, and measure 2 to 5 inches across. Single flowers as their name suggests have only one layer of petals, while double flowers have more than one layer; semidoubles have a layer of much smaller petals arranged inside the normal ones.

Colors of the camellia's blooms range from white to many shades of pink and red. One popular variety, 'Chandleri Elegans', even has pink-and-white speckled flowers. Other favorites are 'Adolphe Audussen', with red, semidouble flowers and golden stamens; 'Alba Simplex' and 'Alba Plena' with white single and double flowers respectively; and 'Pink Perfection', with small, pink, double flowers.

The camellia blooms for several weeks between late winter and late spring, the exact timing varying with the variety. Although the plant grows and blooms prolifically in its native habitat, houseplant varieties are difficult to bring to flower. If treated with great care and given ideal conditions, however, the camellia will reward you with an exquisite display.

The main difficulty is that any slight variation in conditions causes the camellia to drop its flower buds. Although it may occasionally seem to drop its buds for no apparent reason, it is less likely to do so if constant conditions of temperature, humidity and watering are maintained. This is not a plant that will tolerate any neglect. Keep the plant always in the same position. Do not move it to another room or to another place in the room. Do not even move it a few inches along the windowsill or turn the pot around. If it is imperative to move the plant for a moment, mark the pot and the surface where it stands so that it can be returned to exactly the same position.

After flowering, the camellia needs to be left to rest. Ideally, move the plant outside for the summer, placing it on a shady balcony or in a cool, sheltered area of the garden. In the garden plunge the pot up to its rim in earth to keep it cool. In fall, bring the plant back into the house well before any risk of frosts. Prune any untidy or lanky shoots at this time to keep the plant compact.

Camellias can be propagated from stem cuttings, but are not easy to grow. Take cuttings 2 to 3 inches long from half-ripe shoots in early summer. Plant them in a mix of equal parts of peat and sand and provide a bottom heat of 55°F to 60°F. Water them with tepid, lime-free water. Be warned, however, that the temperamental camellia does not root easily and propagation really needs specialist equipment and an expert's knowledge and skill.

Given devoted care and attention, *Camellia japonica* bears exquisite white, pink or red blooms.

Glossy leaves make a perfect background to a camellia's blooms.

GREEN THUMB GUIDE

Watering and feeding

Water the camellia regularly at the same time of day and in similar amounts. Use tepid, soft water – a pH factor of 5.5 is recommended. Water daily throughout the flowering period and into late summer, making sure that the plant remains evenly damp. Slightly decrease the amount of water given in fall, gradually increasing it again toward the flowering period. Never allow the plant to dry out, and never let it become waterlogged. Good drainage is essential.

Feed with water-soluble fertilizer every two or three weeks throughout the growing period. Stop feeding as soon as the flower buds appear or they may drop.

Light and temperature

Bright, cool conditions are essential if the camellia is to form flower buds and keep them through to flowering. Site the pot in a good light, preferably at an east-facing window where the sun's rays will not be too strong. If a south- or west-facing window is the only position where the plant can receive sufficient light, provide adequate shade from the sun.

Keep the plant cool, with a temperature between 45°F and 55°F (60°F is the maximum) until the end of the flowering period. After flowering, keep the plant at an even lower temperature until it can be taken outside for the summer.

It is as important to keep the temperature constant as it is to keep it low. Variations in temperature cause the plant to drop its buds.

Soil and repotting

Camellias need a well-draining, lime-free soil with a pH factor of 5.5. Use a mix of equal parts of loam, peat moss and sand. Repot after flowering, but only when the plant clearly requires it. Always use fresh soil for repotting.

Bellflower
CAMPANULA ISOPHYLLA

An easy-to-grow trailing plant, the bellflower or star of Bethlehem (*Campanula isophylla*) produces a profusion of pretty, star-shaped flowers from midsummer through fall. This dwarf species, popular as a houseplant, comes from the mountainous, limestone regions of northern Italy and is one of the many campanulas that grow wild in Mediterranean countries.

Although the campanula grows only about 6 inches high, its tangled, trailing stems may be 12 to 18 inches long and the plant spreads up to 18 inches. Its pretty leaves are heart-shaped, with slightly serrated edges, and are about half-an-inch across. One variety, 'Mayii', has unusual, slightly hairy leaves with cream markings.

A mature plant bears hundreds of flowers and may remain in bloom until as late as November. The pale blue flowers cluster at the tips of the stems, their open-bell shapes forming inch-wide stars. The variety *C. i.* 'Albi' has white flowers. Also popular are *C. eletines*, with deep blue flowers, and *C. fragilis*, with mid-blue, white-centered blossoms.

Make the most of the campanula's trailing flower-laden stems by placing the plant in a hanging basket or on a pedestal or upturned container. It also makes a stunning display planted in a window-box or balcony tub so that its luxuriant growth can tumble over the edge of its container. Combine some white and blue varieties for a particularly fresh and pretty effect.

Campanula is not a demanding plant, and provided it has plenty of light and reasonable warmth and humidity it will thrive. Keep pinching off dead blooms to help prolong the flowering period.

When it has finished flowering, immediately cut it back and keep it at a temperature of 50°F to 55°F. Provide as much light as possible through the winter, using artificial light as well if necessary. Campanulas do not always survive the winter, however, and even if they do, can be difficult to bring to flower again. If the plant survives through until March, cut it back a further 2 or 3 inches and move it into a temperature of 60°F to 68°F.

Propagate campanulas from seed or stem cuttings, preferably taken from overwintered plants. Take cuttings about 2 inches long in spring. Plant them in a moist mixture of equal parts of peat and sand and keep at about 65°F until rooted. Repot the cuttings individually into 3-inch pots.

GREEN THUMB GUIDE

Watering and feeding
Water campanulas generously during their growing and flowering seasons, April through October. Give extra water on particularly hot, dry days. Do not allow the plant to become waterlogged, however, and do not leave any unabsorbed water in the drip tray. Too much water around the roots is liable to cause any one of a number of fungal diseases that can quickly ruin the plant.

Water overwintering plants sparingly, giving just enough water to keep the potting mix damp.

Feed with water-soluble fertilizer every two weeks. From June through to the end of the flowering period, replace the fertilizer with a high potash feed.

Light and temperature
At home in the strong sunlight of the Mediterranean region, campanulas need as much bright light as possible. They do like the warmth of the sun, but should not be exposed to too much direct sun in midsummer. A good site is an east- or west-facing window where the plant is not exposed to the sun's strongest rays. Overwintering plants also need plenty of light; if necessary, natural light should be supplemented with artificial light to bring the daily total up to about fourteen hours.

Campanulas need warmth, and the more constant the temperature the better. Temperatures of 60°F to 70°F are ideal, but in higher temperatures the plant may start to wilt. Keep humidity high particularly in summer, when a moist atmosphere helps to counteract excessive heat. Place the plant pot on a dish of moist pebbles, but do not allow excess water to stand in the dish.

Soil and repotting
Use a free-draining, loam-based or sandy soil. Never allow the soil to become waterlogged. Repot young plants into progressively larger pots up to about 5 inches.

A wild flower in Mediterranean regions, the campanula needs plenty of bright light when grown indoors. A hanging basket shows off the trailing, flower-laden stems of this white variety, *Campanula isophylla* 'Alba', to best advantage.

In full bloom, the Italian bellflower or star of Bethlehem (*Campanula isophylla*) is a mass of blue, star-shaped flowers. The plant should continue to bear flowers from midsummer until late fall.

Ornamental chili

CAPSICUM ANNUUM

The ornamental peppers, which are related to the large-fruiting, culinary varieties, are decorative plants, grown for their glossy, colorful fruits rather than their flowers. Despite their attractive appearance, the fruits of houseplant varieties of *Capsicum annuum*, known as the Christmas pepper, the ornamental chili and the red pepper plant, are extremely hot and bitter and should not be eaten. There are about 50 species of capsicums, all members of the Solanaceae family.

C. annuum is a bushy plant that grows to a height of about 10 to 18 inches, with a spread of 12 to 15 inches. Its oval leaves are mid-green and 1 to $1\frac{1}{2}$ inches long. The plant is short-lived and is usually grown as an annual to be discarded when fruiting is finished.

Tiny, white, star-shaped flowers with yellow stamens at their centers appear in summer. They measure only about $\frac{1}{2}$ inch across. In late summer or fall, when the plant is some six to eight months old, the flowers are followed by numerous fruits. These cone-shaped, miniature peppers are just 1 to 2 inches long; they are held upright in clusters at the tips of shoots. As they gradually ripen, the fruits change from green to yellow to brilliant red. A single plant may bear fruit at different stages of ripeness and be adorned with all these colors at one time.

The capsicum fruits are long-lasting, but when eventually they start to drop and the leaves shrivel it is time to discard the plant. Keep some fruits for propagating new plants from seed.

Many capsicum hybrids are available, with round, oblong, or even twisting fruits. 'Chameleon' bears fruit that turns from green to white then to purple and red; the fruits of 'Variegated flash' are creamy-white at first, changing to purple. Many varieties are grown to produce their fruit in winter, providing a much-needed splash of color at a time when few plants are in flower.

Pepper plants are readily available in flower stores and garden centers. Buy a young plant when it is in flower or is bearing very small fruit. Its needs are simple: a place at a bright, sunny window, moderate temperatures and high humidity. If kept in a hot dry atmosphere, the plant will not thrive and its fruit will drop off. In these conditions, also, aphids and red spider mites will be attracted to the plant. Mist the leaves daily to discourage such pests.

Capsicums are not easy to propagate at home. Seeds must have warmth to germinate and seedlings are more likely to survive if grown in a warm greenhouse. It can be fun to try, however.

Dry the fruits kept from the old plant and shake out their seeds. Sow in small peat pots containing standard seed mix. Cover the pots with plastic bags to keep humidity high, and set them in a light, warm place – temperatures of 68°F to 72°F are ideal. If the seeds germinate, wait until the seedlings establish some growth and then plant the peat pots in larger pots filled with standard potting mix. Water the young plants just enough to keep the soil moist and treat with care until they are sturdy enough to be treated as mature plants.

GREEN THUMB GUIDE

Watering and feeding
Water generously, but soil should not be soggy. A plant in an earthenware pot benefits from occasional immersion in a bowl of water.

While the fruits are developing, feed every two weeks with water-soluble fertilizer. As soon as the fruits start to show some color, stop feeding or they will drop.

Light and temperature
Make sure a capsicum gets plenty of light and sunshine. This is one plant that can not only tolerate, but thrives on, direct sunshine. Nevertheless, the plant should be kept in rooms of average temperature – 70°F, with an absolute
minimum of 50°F. If the temperature is too high, the leaves will fall and the fruits will first lose their color, then drop.

Mist the leaves daily and set a dish of moistened pebbles under the plant to increase humidity.

Soil and repotting
Use a standard potting mix for mature plants and for seedlings. Plants are discarded after fruiting and do not need repotting.

The ornamental chili (*Capsicum annuum*) is grown for
its colorful, long-lasting fruits.

Madagascar periwinkle
CATHARANTHUS ROSEUS

A handsome plant with glossy leaves and rose-pink flowers, the Madagascar periwinkle (*Catharanthus roseus*) does come from the island of its name, where it grows as a low bush. It is a member of the Apocynaceae family and is also known as *Vinca rosea*.

Grown as a houseplant, the Madagascar periwinkle reaches a height of about 14 inches. Its shiny, oval leaves are about 2 inches long and dark-green in color, with light veins.

The plant blooms profusely from late spring through fall, bearing pretty pink flowers with darker pink centers; each bloom is about 1 to 1½ inches across. Some attractive varieties are 'Little Pinkie', with pink flowers, and 'Little Bright Eye', which bears white blooms with pink centers. Grow several varieties together to create a lovely display of massed flowers.

The hardy periwinkle (*Vinca major*) comes from the same family as the Madagascar periwinkle. A popular garden plant, it is a more common and sturdier plant than its indoor relative. The houseplant, however, bears the more beautiful flowers.

Catharanthus is not a difficult plant to grow but it needs plenty of light and sun. It also prefers a humid atmosphere – in its native home it grows in rain forests – and regular misting helps prolong the flowering period.

Although it is evergreen and can survive through the winter, the catharanthus is unlikely to flower successfully a second year. It is usually grown as an annual and then discarded. Since these can be difficult plants to find, however, it is well worth keeping the periwinkle through the winter, and taking cuttings to propagate your own plants for the following summer. Overwinter the plant at a temperature of 50°F to 60°F and be sure to keep its soil moist. The plant may lose leaves and become scrawny but is still able to provide perfectly healthy cuttings.

To propagate a catharanthus, take 3-inch cuttings from young shoots in spring or early summer. Plant them in pots filled with sandy soil and, ideally, keep at a temperature of about 60°F. Cuttings planted in a heated propagating frame will root more readily. Transfer rooted cuttings to 3-inch pots containing sandy soil. Pinch out the growing tips to encourage bushy growth and repot into larger pots when necessary.

Catharanthus can also be grown from seed. In March, sow seeds in trays of standard seed mix and keep at a temperature of about 60°F. After three or four weeks, when the seedlings are large enough to handle, transfer them to individual small pots, or plant several together in a larger pot. Use fresh standard potting mix. As for plants grown from cuttings, pinch out the growing tips to encourage an attractive bushy shape.

GREEN THUMB GUIDE

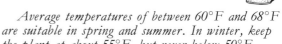
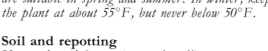

Watering and feeding
Regular watering encourages profuse flowering. If the plant is allowed to dry out, even for a short while, there will be a break in flowering. Keep the soil moist by watering frequently, daily in summer. In winter, water just enough to keep the soil damp.

In summer, feed plants every two weeks with dilute water-soluble fertilizer.

Light and temperature
A sunny windowsill is the ideal position for catharanthus. Shade the plant from the hottest sun, however, and mist the leaves frequently, particularly in hot, dry weather.

Average temperatures of between 60°F and 68°F are suitable in spring and summer. In winter, keep the plant at about 55°F, but never below 50°F.

Soil and repotting
Use sandy soil for cuttings and seedlings. Catharanthus is rarely worth keeping for a second year so does not require repotting.

The Madagascar periwinkle (*Catharanthus roseus*)
blooms its best in warm, humid conditions.

Plume flower

CELOSIA ARGENTEA PLUMOSA

Colorful, plumelike flowers are typical of *Celosia argentea plumosa*, commonly known as the plume flower. One of a genus of 60 species, all of which produce showy feathery or crested flowers, it is a member of the Amaranthaceae family and comes from tropical Asia.

Flowering usually begins in May and continues through the summer. The silky, conical celosia flowerheads appear at the top of the plant and may be brilliant red, pink, apricot or golden-yellow and up to 9 inches long. Leaves are pale- to mid-green, oval in shape and up to 4 inches long.

Standard plants grow to a height of about 2 feet, but there are dwarf varieties of the plants such as 'Golden Plume' and 'Kewpie' which reach only 8 to 12 inches. One dwarf variety, 'Fairy Fountains', produces magnificent plumes of flowers in a wide range of colors. Varieties of *C. cristata* bear crestlike flowers or "cockscombs." These blooms may be red, orange or yellow and measure up to 5 inches across (see p. 67).

Usually grown outdoors as a bedding plant, the celosia can grow well as a houseplant, given the right conditions. It needs plenty of light, moderate temperatures and good ventilation – sunrooms and greenhouses are ideal situations for this plant.

Celosia can be raised from seed, but a nursery-reared plant is likely to be stronger and produce better flowers. The plant rarely flowers well a second year, so is usually discarded after flowering. If you want to keep the plant, cut it back in fall and care for it through the winter, or transfer it outside to the yard or garden.

If you wish to try growing plants from seed, sow them in February or March in trays or pans of seed mix. Keep at a temperature of 60°F to 65°F. Once seedlings are large enough to handle, prick them out into boxes filled with a fresh peat-based mix. Leave them to grow for a few weeks then repot in fresh, peat-based soil, placing two or three in a 4-inch pot. Once growth is well-established, treat as mature plants.

Celosias are highly susceptible to fungal diseases which rot their roots and can eventually lead to the plants' collapse. Always use fresh, clean potting mix when dealing with these plants at any stage. Never use soil in which another plant has been growing and never use soil from the garden. Either could contain parasitic fungi.

The silky, feathery blooms of the aptly-named plume flower appear through the summer, provided the plant has plenty of light, sun and water.

GREEN THUMB GUIDE

Watering and feeding

Water the plume flower as often as necessary to keep the soil thoroughly moist. In winter, give less water, just enough to keep the soil damp. Never let the plant dry out.

During the period of active growth feed every two weeks with dilute water-soluble fertilizer.

Light and temperature

Celosia needs plenty of bright light and some sunshine; shade it from the strong summer sun. Keep humidity high by misting the leaves occasionally, particularly in hot weather.

If the plant is to produce large, abundant blooms, it must be kept at a temperature of 50°F to 60°F, with good ventilation.

Soil

Use a standard, peat-based mix. Always make sure that soil is fresh and clean – this plant is susceptible to fungal infections.

The plume flower (*Celosia argentea plumosa*) bears
dramatic red or yellow blooms, which rise above its
pale-green leaves.

Chrysanthemum

CHRYSANTHEMUM MORIFOLIUM

Originally a native of China and Japan, the chrysanthemum had a religious significance in ancient China and is still much used today as a motif in paintings and fabrics, as a garnish for food and in the popular chrysanthemum tea. In 500 A.D. the plant was made the imperial flower of Japan. The chrysanthemum was first brought to Europe at the end of the seventeenth century, when it was an extremely costly item for the wealthy enthusiast only, and from where it reached North America. Today, inexpensive, profusely-flowering chrysanthemum plants can be bought all year round.

The potted chrysanthemums now sold, ready to flower, are the result of many years' specialized cultivation and are somewhat artificial. Hormone dwarfing compounds are applied to prevent plants reaching their full natural height and keep them a manageable size for indoor use. Other techniques are used to bring the plants into flower at all seasons.

Hundreds of varieties of pot chrysanthemums have been developed with flowers in every imaginable shade of red, purple, pink, orange, bronze and yellow, as well as white and cream. The round heavy flowerheads are many-petaled and take a variety of different forms. These include flowers with incurving, tightly packed petals, flowers with spiky petals and others resembling pompoms. Some bear a single, large bloom to a stem; others, the spray chrysanthemums, bear many flowers to a stem. The distinctive, dark-green leaves are from 3 to 5 inches long.

A highly popular chrysanthemum that is sometimes grown indoors is the Marguerite chrysanthemum (*C. frutescens*) which bears single, daisylike white or pale-yellow flowers. The simple freshness of this beautiful plant will brighten any interior. The cascade chrysanthemums can also be grown in pots. Their trailing stems bear a mass of small, pretty flowers.

Pot chrysanthemums are easy to obtain. Choose a plant with some open flowers and lots of buds that are starting to show color. Buds that are still all green or have black centers may fail to open.

These plants grow well indoors, particularly if they receive good light and plenty of water. Pick off dead flowers regularly and the plant should continue to bloom for up to two months. If the leaves wilt, the most likely reason is lack of water. If the flowering season is short, the plant has probably been kept at too high a temperature, and if the buds do not open at all, the plant may have been an unhealthy specimen with green buds to begin with, or has received insufficient light.

Aphids and red spider mites may attack pot chrysanthemums, particularly in hot, dry weather. Keep the plants in moderate temperatures if possible, and mist their leaves regularly.

Once the plant has finished flowering do not try to keep it for a second indoor flowering season. It will now revert to its normal height and flowering time, a process that can only be prevented by the techniques of the professional grower. Plant it outside, and it will flower the following fall if it is a hardy variety.

Propagation, too, is best left to the nursery. While outdoor plants can be grown easily, indoor varieties need the special conditions which restrict their height and regulate their flowering time.

GREEN THUMB GUIDE

Watering and feeding

Keep the chrysanthemum's soil moist. Water as often as necessary, which may be several days a week or even daily in hot weather.

Feed with dilute water-soluble fertilizer only while the flowers are in bud. As soon as they start to open, stop feeding. Since most plants are purchased with some blooms already open, feeding is rarely necessary.

Light and temperature

The pot chrysanthemum needs plenty of light if it is to flower well. An east- or west-facing window is ideal, but give the plant some shade from hot sun. If set at a south-facing window, the plant must be screened from the sun by a sheer curtain. Mist the leaves regularly and in hot, dry weather set the pot on a tray of moist pebbles.

A temperature of 68°F is comfortable for the plant. It will survive temperatures down to 40°F.

Soil and repotting

The plant is bought ready-potted in the rich soil it needs. Do not try to repot and keep for a second indoor flowering but, if possible, transfer the plant to a garden flowerbed.

Pot chrysanthemums are grown to flower at all times
of year. They bloom for up to two months, bearing
flowers in a wide range of colors.

Bleeding-heart vine

CLERODENDRUM THOMSONIAE

The bleeding-heart vine (*Clerodendrum thomsoniae*) comes from West Africa where it grows as a climbing plant up to a height of 12 feet. A member of the Verbenaceae family, it is one of a genus of 400 or so flowering plants, which come mostly from tropical regions.

Grown indoors, a clerodendrum can be kept to a manageable size of 2 or 3 feet by pinching out growing tips and pruning. If space allows, however, a large plant can form a dramatic focal point for a large area. This is one of the most decorative of all flowering plants, and it looks especially attractive in a hanging basket.

The bleeding-heart vine's large, deep-green leaves are of a pointed, oval shape. Its clusters of striking, pendulous flowers appear in abundance from late spring through summer. Each flower is red and white, the star-shaped, crimson central part surrounded by the billowing white "petals" of the calyx. (They are really sepals, not petals.) After flowering, the plant produces trailing stems up to 3 feet long.

C. speciosissimum and *C. paniculatum* are also magnificent plants. Both have heart-shaped leaves and large clusters of scarlet flowers.

The clerodendrum is not an easy plant to grow and probably does best in a greenhouse. Indoors, set it in an average room temperature, and provide it with plenty of light and high humidity. A sunroom or greenhouse is an ideal home for this gracious plant, but it must be shaded from strong direct sun.

Mist the plant frequently – it is a jungle dweller and needs humid air. Humidity also discourages the attacks from aphids and red spider mites to which the plant is susceptible. Always use lime-free water, however, since the plant is prone to chlorosis, an iron and manganese deficiency exacerbated by the presence of lime. Chlorosis causes the leaves to turn yellow and mottled and thus ruins the health and appearance of the plant.

Once flowering has finished, prune the plant to encourage new growth the following year, then allow it to rest from October through February. Clerodendrums are not particularly sturdy plants and do not always survive through the winter. Improve your plant's chances by placing it in a cool position where it will receive plenty of winter sunshine. In spring, prune again lightly, removing any straggly stems and pinching out growing tips to maintain the plant's attractive shape.

This is a difficult plant to propagate at home. If you wish to try, take cuttings of about 3 to 4 inches in length from side shoots in spring. Plant them in a mix of equal parts of peat and sand, and provide gentle bottom heat. Cuttings planted in a heated propagating case have the best chance of success. If they root, plant them in individual 3-inch pots in loam-based soil and treat with care. Once growth is well-established, repot the new plants as necessary.

The bleeding heart vine (*Clerodendrum thomsoniae*) is an elegant climber that can reach a height of 12 feet. Pruning keeps it to a more manageable size for indoor display. Clusters of delicate red and white flowers adorn the plant in summer and may bloom from May through September. Their coloring is perfectly complemented by the attractive white container used for this particular specimen.

GREEN THUMB GUIDE

Watering and feeding
Water generously while the plant is in flower, daily if necessary in hot weather. Do not allow the plant to dry out during the flowering period or the blooms will fall. Always use lime-free water for misting and watering, since the plant is susceptible to chlorosis. Water more sparingly in winter while the plant is resting, allowing the soil partially to dry out between waterings.

Feed with water-soluble fertilizer every ten days or so during the spring and summer growing season. In winter, feed once every four weeks.

Light and temperature
Clerodendrums need strong light while actively growing, but cannot tolerate hot summer sunshine. The weaker rays of the winter sun, however, are beneficial during the plant's resting period.

An average room temperature of 60°F to 68°F is suitable for most of the year. In winter, keep the plant at 55°F to 60°F, never below 50°F.

Soil and repotting
Use a gritty, loam-based soil containing three parts of regular potting mix and one part of sand. Repot young vigorous plants every spring. Older, slower-growing plants should be repotted only when really necessary. Select a pot that is just a little small relative to the plant's height. This will prevent the clerodendrum from growing too big and unwieldy.

Kaffir lily

CLIVIA MINIATA

Popularly known as the Kaffir lily, *Clivia miniata* bears spectacular clusters of flowers at the top of fleshy stalks. Despite its name this South African plant is not a lily but a member of the Amaryllidaceae family. Its leaves and flowers are mildly poisonous and can cause a slight skin rash on contact.

The leathery straplike leaves of the clivia are dark green and between 1½ and 3 inches wide; they grow to a length of up to 24 inches. New leaves appear every summer and an equivalent number are lost the following winter. Clusters of bell-shaped flowers are borne on fleshy stalks, rising from the center of the leaves, and bloom from early spring through summer. Each cluster holds up to 20 flowers, all 2 to 3 inches long. Brilliant orange is the usual flower color, but there are some red and yellow varieties.

When flowering is finished, cut off the flowerheads. Leave the stalk to wither, then gently pull it out.

While clivias are not demanding plants, they do need more care than is sometimes thought. It is essential for the clivia to rest in winter. It will not flower if it is given fertilizer or too much heat or water during this period. A clivia needs space around it and the minimum of disturbance. Do not move the plant when it is in bud or flower and do not repot unless really necessary. A pot-bound clivia is healthier than one with too much space.

Propagate by taking offshoots from an established plant. Set them in 5-inch pots and water sparingly until the roots have taken. When an old plant in a 10- or 12-inch pot is extremely overcrowded, take it out of the pot and carefully divide the roots. Plant each section in its own 5-inch pot and keep at about 60°F until established.

GREEN THUMB GUIDE

Watering and feeding
Water the clivia moderately through the active growth period, just enough to keep the soil evenly damp. In fall and during the plant's winter rest, give only enough water to keep the soil from drying out. Start to increase the watering again when the flower stalk is 4 to 6 inches long.

Feed once or twice a month during the growing season with dilute water-soluble fertilizer. Do not feed in winter.

Light and temperature
Set the clivia in good light, but shade it from direct sun in summer. The plant likes humidity so place a tray of damp pebbles under the pot to moisten the atmosphere. Sponge the leaves occasionally, too.

Temperatures of 60°F to 70°F are suitable for most of the year. Overwinter the plant at between 45°F and 50°F.

Soil and repotting
Loam-based soil suits clivias best. Repot in early spring, but only if the plant is totally pot-bound. In fact a plant that is pot-bound flowers better than one with too much space around its roots. Use a pot only slightly larger than the previous one so that the roots still occupy most of the space.

Propagating clivias
1 Choose offsets with at least 3 leaves about 8 inches long.
2 Using a sharp knife, cut carefully through the point where the offset joins the parent plant.
3 Repot individual offsets in a humus-rich potting mix in 3-inch pots. Keep the soil just moist, allowing the top two-thirds to dry out between waterings. Move to larger pots when the roots appear on the surface.

A well-tended clivia lives for many years, producing
yearly clusters of orange-red flowers.

Columnea

COLUMNEA GLORIOSA

Magnificent trailing plants, columneas grow in the tropical rain forests of South America. They are epiphytes – they do not root in the soil but lodge themselves high on the branches of forest trees. The genus contains about 200 species and belongs to the Gesneriaceae family.

C. gloriosa comes from Costa Rica and, given the right conditions, will flower indoors year after year. Its trailing stems are 2 to 4 feet long and bear closely set pairs of tiny leaves. These leaves, only $\frac{3}{4}$ inch long, are covered with fine reddish hairs. From October through April the plant produces an abundance of delicate, tubular flowers that are fiery-red in color with yellow throats.

Some other attractive varieties are *C. g.* 'Purpurea' which has purplish leaves, and 'Yellow dragon' which bears bright yellow flowers. *C. schiedeana*, from Mexico, has scarlet flowers flecked with yellow or brown which bloom from May to July. The glossy-leaved *C. × banksii* bears orange-red flowers and is said to be one of the easier columneas to grow. Some columneas flower in winter, some in summer.

C. gloriosa needs high humidity, plenty of water and light, but not direct sun. Set the pot on an east-facing windowsill so that its stems trail downward, but give some shade when the sun gains strength. The plant perhaps looks its best in a hanging basket or raised on a pedestal to show off its pendulous stems and attractive flowers to the full.

To keep humidity as high as this rain forest plant demands, mist the leaves daily, twice a day in hot weather. Take the plant into a steamy bathroom or laundry room for an hour or two. Damp peat moss packed around the pot helps maintain high humidity as does a sphagnum moss lining to a hanging basket.

If the plant starts to drop its leaves, something is wrong. The commonest cause is too dry an atmosphere. If humidity is high, check that the plant is not in a draft, that it has not been under- or over-watered and that the temperature has not fallen too low.

When the plant has finished flowering, cut back any weak or overlong stems and cut out dead growth.

Propagate *C. gloriosa* by stem cuttings. Take cuttings about 3 inches in length in spring and plant in a mixture of equal parts of peat and sand. Use a propagating case heated to about 65°F or, if the cuttings are planted in pots, cover them with plastic bags to maintain humidity and keep warm. When the cuttings have rooted, repot them into 3-inch pots containing a standard potting mix with some additional peat moss. Once the plants are growing vigorously, pinch out growing tips to encourage bushy growth. Cutting-grown plants can be potted on to larger pots when necessary or transferred, several at a time, to hanging baskets.

Although *Columnea gloriosa* can be difficult to bring to bloom, it rewards good care by producing a mass of fiery flowers year after year.

GREEN THUMB GUIDE

Watering and feeding
Water generously in summer, keeping the potting mix moist at all times. Give water more sparingly in winter, but never let the plant dry out. Always use tepid, lime-free water.

Feed weekly with dilute water-soluble fertilizer while the plant is actively growing. Stop feeding as soon as the flower buds appear.

Light and temperature
C. gloriosa needs plenty of bright light but cannot tolerate direct sunshine, except for the weaker rays of the early morning sun. For this reason an east-facing window is best, but make sure the plant is shaded when necessary.

C. gloriosa *flowers in winter when it needs a minimum temperature of 60°F to 70°F. Keep it as cool as possible in summer. Summer-flowering columneas should be kept at 50°F to 55°F through the winter to allow them to rest. Keep humidity high and mist the leaves regularly.*

Soil and repotting
Use a standard potting mix, but add a little peat moss. In hanging baskets, use a well-draining mix of equal parts of soilless potting mix and sphagnum moss. Repot C. gloriosa in summer before new growth starts in fall. Older plants should need repotting only every other year.

Root trimming

It is not always necessary to move potbound plants on to larger pots. If columnea roots outgrow the pot you wish to keep the plant in, simply trim away the bottom third of the root ball. Return the plant to its original pot with some new mix.

Firecracker flower

CROSSANDRA INFUNDIBULIFORMIS

A low-growing evergreen shrub, the firecracker flower (*Crossandra infundibuliformis*) comes from eastern India and Sri Lanka where it thrives in the monsoon forests. Now a popular houseplant, its fine, long-lasting flowers make it a welcome addition to any indoor garden. One of a genus of 50 species of evergreen plants, it belongs to the Acanthaceae family.

Grown as a houseplant, the firecracker flower may reach a height of up to 3 feet and a spread of 2 feet. Its dark-green leaves, each about 4 inches in length, are glossy and slightly leathery in texture, with wavy edges. Salmon-pink to orange flowers are borne on short, upward-growing spikes above the leaves. Each flower is composed of a slender tube which splays out into five rounded lobes, the lower three of which are slightly enlarged, forming a pronounced "lip."

An African species of *Crossandra*, *C. nilotica*, grows to a height of about 2 feet and bears unusual brick-red flowers.

The flowering season can extend from March to November. New plants grown from seed may be only a few months old when they start to flower. Although some crossandras flower well year after year, better blooms are usually obtained from young plants. Use an overwintered specimen for taking cuttings.

The crossandra needs plenty of light and, above all, a high level of humidity if it is to bear abundant blooms over a lengthy flowering period. Mist the plant frequently and either set the pot on a tray of damp pebbles or surround it with moist peat. If conditions become particularly dry, try the following method of increasing humidity. Place an upturned saucer in a deep bowl, stand the plant on the saucer and water up to, but not touching, the pot.

Also try grouping the crossandra with other plants so that it can benefit from the moisture given off by their leaves. Place individually potted plants in one large container, or grow them all in the same large pot.

In spring, prune the plant lightly, removing any straggly untidy stems. Overwintered plants will usually have lost some leaves, but take off some top growth to encourage bushiness.

Propagate by stem cuttings taken in spring. Plant the 2- to 3-inch cuttings in 3-inch pots containing a mix of peat and sand. Cover the pots with plastic bags to retain humidity and keep warm. Alternatively use a heated propagating case. Once the cuttings have rooted, repot as necessary into progressively larger pots until the plants are in 8-inch pots.

Crossandra plants can also be grown from seed. Sow seeds in March and keep at a temperature of about 60°F until germinated. Transplant the seedlings to pots when large enough to handle.

GREEN THUMB GUIDE

Watering and feeding

Water the firecracker flower generously throughout the growing and flowering seasons, keeping the potting mix moist. Water more sparingly in winter, giving just enough to keep the soil from drying out. Increase watering again in spring for overwintered plants.

Mist the plant frequently and follow suggestions above for maintaining the high humidity so essential to this plant. Always use tepid, lime-free water for watering and misting.

Feed with dilute water-soluble fertilizer every two weeks from spring through summer.

Light and temperature

Crossandras need plenty of bright light if they are to flower well but cannot tolerate strong summer sun. Site the plant at an east- or west-facing window and shade from the hottest rays of the sun with a sheer curtain.

If overwintering a plant, give it as much light as possible from September through May.

In summer keep the plant in temperatures of 60°F to 70°F. In winter the temperature should not fall below 55°F.

Soil and repotting

Repot an overwintered plant in spring if necessary. Use a standard peat-based potting mix, with the addition of one quarter part of sand.

The firecracker flower's orange-pink blooms may last
from March through November.

Cyclamen
CYCLAMEN PERSICUM

One of the finest of flowering houseplants, the cyclamen is justifiably popular, despite being a difficult plant to grow in the home. Nevertheless, cyclamens are worth all the attention they demand, for their flowers offer a rare combination of flamboyance and daintiness, the decorative leaves are an attraction in their own right and the plants flower for up to three months in winter. New hybrids bloom almost year-round.

A member of the Primulaceae family, the cyclamen grows wild in parts of North Africa, Mediterranean countries and the Middle East.

As a houseplant the standard cyclamen grows to a height of 9 to 12 inches; dwarf varieties are 7 inches or less. The thick green leaves are heart-shaped with intricate markings; those of *C. persicum* are dark-green, subtly patterned in silver and gray. The delicate flowers have sharply curved-back, or reflexed petals. Held high on long stalks, they seem to hover like beautiful butterflies above the foliage. The flowers of *C. persicum* and varieties are white, salmon-pink, rose-pink, red, purple or lilac-colored.

Popular cyclamen varieties include 'Ruffled' which has fringed flowers in pink, red and mauve; the early-flowering 'Firmament', and 'Rex', noted for its silver-marbled leaves.

When buying a cyclamen, choose a plant with plenty of buds: buds showing some color are more likely to flower than those that are still green. Keep the plant in a light, cool, airy position, away from any source of heating. Remove any dead leaves or flowers by gently twisting them off the stems; cutting them could lead to a rotted corm.

If something is wrong in its environment, the cyclamen usually lets you know. Yellowing leaves indicate too little water, too much exposure to sunlight or too high a temperature. Dropping leaves warn of underwatering, while rotting buds result from too much water. A collapsed plant with a rotting corm points to careless watering that has led to the corm becoming water-logged.

Careless watering is also the cause of gray leaf mold (botrytis) which can develop when water droplets become trapped between leaf and flower stem. Cyclamens are also susceptible to infestation by red spider mites and aphids.

If your cyclamen manages to negotiate these problems and rewards lavish care with a prolonged flowering season, allow it to rest when flowering ceases. Reduce the amount of water given until all the leaves are wilted, then leave the pot on its side in a cool place. In July, repot the plant and keep cool and in good light until new growth begins.

Cyclamen are propagated from seed and the period from seeding to flowering can be as long as 18 months. Sow seeds in spring or summer in standard seed mix. Once seedlings are established, transfer them to 4-inch pots containing a mix of three parts standard potting mix to one part of coarse sand. Move to 5-inch pots when the corms begin to need more space.

GREEN THUMB GUIDE

Watering and feeding
Water sparingly, allowing the soil to become almost – but never completely – dry between waterings. Never leave any excess water in or around the pot; this can cause the corm to rot and the consequent death of the plant. Take care, too, not to let the leaves, shoots or corm get wet since this can cause fungal disease or rot. Trickle water very gently around the rim of the pot or simply stand the pot in tepid water for a minute or two. Always use tepid, lime-free water.

Feed growing plants with dilute water-soluble fertilizer every two weeks. Strong, full-grown plants do not need feeding, and never feed a plant that is flowering or in bud.

Light and temperature
Good light is essential but do not leave the plant in direct sun. A north-facing window is probably the best position for a cyclamen.

Temperatures below 65°F but with a minimum of 40°F are ideal. The cyclamen needs some humidity but should not be misted since this may damage the corm. If the air is particularly dry, stand the pot on moist pebbles or surround it with damp moss.

Soil and repotting
Repot after flowering and at the end of the summer. Use a fresh potting mix containing three parts of standard mix to one part of coarse sand each time. Always leave half the corm exposed above the soil.

Classic white containers enhance the simple beauty of
a white cyclamen.

Although famed for its flowers, the cyclamen also has large, attractively marbled leaves that are a delight in themselves.

Deadheading a cyclamen
To maintain robust and healthy plants, as well as for aesthetic reasons, remove faded flowers and yellowing leaves from cyclamens. Take out the entire offending stalk by twisting the stem at its base and giving a sharp tug.

Held aloft on their long stems, the cyclamen's
delicate flowers, with their dainty swept-back petals,
seem almost to hover above the foliage.

A healthy plant: at-a-glance fitness test

Flowers should exhibit a healthy vigor and good color. Reject a plant with wilting or blotched blooms, which result from lack of feeding.

Buds should be firm and healthy looking. Reject a plant with black buds (possibly due to over-dry atmosphere or red spider mite) or shriveled, distorted buds caused by viral or insect attack.

Stems should be erect and sturdy. Reject plants with wilting stems (if necessary remove protective wrapper to check) or stems showing signs of mildew. Check the base for signs of stem rot.

Leaves should be sturdy and robust. Reject plants with leaves that are going brown at the edges or have turned yellow. Blotchy, mottled, moldy or curling leaves indicate viral, insect or fungal infections.

Undersides of leaves should be closely examined for signs of insect infestation.

BUYING NEW PLANTS

Indoor gardeners may obtain new plants from a variety of sources, ranging from the local supermarket to specialist nurseries. As a general rule it is best to purchase from commercial outlets whose expertise and quality control you can trust. Although there is a lot to be said for the resilience of any plant that can withstand the neglect it is subject to on most supermarket shelves, it makes better sense to buy only from retailers who obviously have the plants' best interest at heart.

It is usually possible to make a quick judgment of whether or not the plants on sale have been well cared for. If they are displayed outside in the cold, if they are kept in protective wrappers that inhibit watering, if they are standing on capillary matting which has dried out – they are not likely to be in the best of health.

Taking a diseased specimen into your home will jeopardize your entire collection of indoor plants, so be prepared to be hyper-critical

in your assessment of a plant before buying – and be ready to pay for quality.

The drawing above shows the most important features to check. Do not be timid about subjecting plants to close scrutiny – ask for protective wrappings to be removed. Regard any disapproval by the storekeeper as a warning signal. An apparently healthy and robust cyclamen, for example, might wilt alarmingly once its supportive packaging is withdrawn.

When purchasing a flowering plant it is sensible to opt for a specimen with plenty of good healthy looking buds about to open, rather than one which is already in full bloom and thus nearing the end of its flowering period. And since many indoor flowering plants are bought for their decorative and colorful contribution to a particular setting, make sure that the situation you have in mind for a particular plant will indeed meet its needs for light, warmth and humidity. If you have

any doubts about this, an experienced retailer should be able to advise you.

What's in a name?

Any serious gardener, indoors or out, will find it useful to know about the botanical as well as the popular names of plants. Knowing a plant's Latin name will help identify it correctly in any part of the country – or the world.

Common or popular names vary from country to country and may also vary from one region to another. In North America, for example, hemlock is the name of a huge coniferous tree, whose Latin name is *Tsuga canadensis*. In Britain, by contrast, hemlock is a poisonous weed, Latin name *Conium maculatum*. So although "divided by a common language" as far as popular names go, there could be no possibility of confusion in the minds of American and English botanists using the plants' scientific names.

All botanical names for plant species consist of two principal parts. This two-word Latin name or "binomial" often reflects the plants' characteristics.

The Latin binomial results from the way in which plants are classified, that is, the way in which they are arranged into groups by specialists known as taxonomists. All members of the plant kingdom thus belong to a family, a genus and a species. Many species are also found in a range of different varieties.

FAMILIES
Plant families are composed of groups of related plant genera. Family names nearly always end in *-aceae* or simply *-ae*. All plants grouped together in the same family have a selection of botanical features in common. Surprisingly, however, this does not necessarily mean that the plants look alike. The potato, tomato and the capsicum, which are superficially dissimilar are all members of the family Solanaceae.

GENERA
Every plant family is composed of many genera, and each genus is composed of many species. The very name genus means "kind," which gives a clue to the way the organization works. In the family Solanaceae, for instance, the cap-

---

A useful vocabulary

album	white	*hortensis*	of gardens
angustifolius	narrow leaved	*majalis*	of the month of May
annuus	annual	*muralis*	of (or on) walls
aquaticus	aquatic	*nanus*	dwarf
argenteus	silvery	*novae angliae*	of New England
australis	southern	*novi-belgii*	of New Belgium
azureus	sky blue		(New York)
blandus	agreeable	*officinalis*	medicinal
borealis	northern	*palmatus*	divided like a hand
brevi-	short	*patens*	spreading
caeruleus	blue	*platy-*	broad
campanulatus	bell shaped	*poly-*	many
candicans	whitish	*pumilus*	dwarf
candidissimus	pure white	*radicans*	rooting
candidus	shining white	*repens*	creeping
cardinalis	red	*rubens*	red
cordatus	heart shaped	*scandens*	climbing
dentatus	sharp toothed	*semperflorens*	ever flowering
edulis	edible	*sempervirens*	evergreen
elatus, elatior	tall	*sinensis*	Chinese
esculentus	edible	*speciosus*	showy
fruticosus	shrubby	*truncatus*	cut off squarely
grandiflorus	large flowered	*vulgaris*	common
grandifolius	large leaved	*zebrinus*	striped

---

sicum belongs to the genus *Capsicum* while the potato is in the genus *Solanum* and the tomato in the genus *Lycopersicon*.

SPECIES
The second part of the binomial is the species name. This second word, sometimes called the "specific epithet" identifies the species. The species is the basic unit of classification, particularly since it is the lowest common denominator of plant reproduction. Plants of the same species can cross (breed) and produce viable offspring; these will set seed which, in turn, will germinate to produce fertile new plants. Plants of the same genus cannot usually do this *unless* they belong to the same species.

The species names of the three examples quoted above are as follows:
Potato: *Solanum tuberosum*
Tomato: *Lycopersicon esculentum*
Capsicum: *Capsicum annuum*.

Plants of the same species are identical in all important aspects such as flower and leaf structure, if

not in precise details such as height and coloration.

VARIETIES
Any slight differences between plants in a particular species – say variegated instead of plain green foliage, white instead of pink flower heads – are indicated by a third, or varietal name. Varieties may be spelled with small letters, or may begin with a capital letter.

CULTIVARS
New plant varieties usually arise "naturally," that is, in the wild. However, many plants reach the form in which they are sold through deliberate manipulation, breeding and selection techniques.

Many years of research and experimentation may go into producing a new "variety" which is different from the original species in size, color or habit. Plants that arise in this way are known as "cultivars." All cultivars are named in their country of origin and they are known by these names throughout the world.

Extending your collection

KANGAROO THORN
Acacia armata
The best known acacia is the perennially popular mimosa, a native of Australia. The kangaroo thorn which also comes from Australia, will develop in the wild into a large bush or small tree 10 feet or more tall. Indoors it will reach 3 or 4 feet.

As its common name suggests (and, indeed its Latin specific name: *armata* = armed, see p. 66) the leaves are prickly. In spring it produces delightful fluffy mimosalike yellow flowers.

The kangaroo thorn will do well in bright light and cool, airy conditions. Keep it only slightly moist in winter and allow it to rest at about 40°F. Increase watering in spring and feed every two weeks in the active growing period. Repot, if necessary, after flowering. Take cuttings in February and March.

BLUE AFRICAN LILY
Agapanthus africanus
This summer-flowering lily, a native of South Africa, actually does better in a container than in the open garden, since it seems to prefer cramped conditions.

Attractive violet-blue clusters of narrow bell-shaped flowers rise on erect stems 2 feet tall from clumps of arching, strap-shaped leaves. If plants are to flower well the following summer, they should be kept dry and cool during the winter resting period (November through April).

Pot in a humus-rich mix and keep in a sunny, south-facing window. Divide, and repot divisions, every 4 years or so.

ZEBRA PLANT
Aphelandra squarrosa
Only two of the eighty species of tropical shrubs and plants in this genus are grown as indoor plants. Both produce glossy, gray-green leaves with broad silvery-white markings. The flowers, which appear in spring, are less interesting than the attractive orange-yellow bracts on which they are borne.

Zebra plants do well in bright light (not direct sun) and can be potted in a standard mix. They should be watered sparingly in the winter resting period – just enough to keep the mix moist. Water frequently in the active growth period and, most important, feed once a week during this time. Allow plants to rest after flowering. Propagate from stem cuttings taken in the spring.

BLOOD FLOWER
Asclepias curassavica
From June through October, this native of tropical South America produces clusters of attractively shaped orange-red flowers. It is from these that the plant's common name is derived.

Indoors, in a standard potting mix, the blood flower will grow to between 2 and 3 feet. In the winter rest period it must be kept cool (it will tolerate temperatures as low as 45°F) and watered only enough to prevent the soil drying out. Increase watering and feed every two weeks from March through October. Plants will benefit from severe pruning in March. Propagate from seed or from young shoot cuttings.

JEWEL PLANT
Bertolonia marmorata
Bertolonias are charming small plants (never growing more than 6 inches tall), whose decorative foliage offsets delicate and simple purple or pink flowers. The large, heart-shaped leaves may grow to 5 or 8 inches in length and in the case of *B. marmorata* have pronounced silvery-white bands on their upper surface. Those of *B. m. aenea* are predominantly copper colored.

Although the plants do well in a humid atmosphere, the leaves

Kangaroo thorn

Blue African lily

Zebra plant

Blood flower

Jewel plant

should not be misted since accumulations of water will cause discoloration of the foliage.

Use a standard potting mix or make one up composed of equal parts leaf mold, peat moss and perlite. Water liberally in the active growth period and sparingly in winter. Feed every two weeks in the growing period.

Repot when the creeping stems have covered the surface of the soil and are growing down the side of the container. Propagate from tip cuttings taken in the early spring.

QUEEN'S TEARS
Billbergia nutans

This is one of the most popular of all the flowering bromeliads (see p. 68), not least because it is a plant of extreme tolerance.

Billbergia's distinctive pink, blue and yellow pendulous flowers emerge from bright pink bracts. The arching, grasslike leaves grow in clusters; each cluster has a "vase" at its center, which must be kept constantly topped up with water.

Any billbergia will do well if it is exposed to 3 or 4 hours' direct sunlight a day. Normal room temperatures will suit them, although *B. nutans* will tolerate winter temperatures as low as 45°F.

Use a standard bromeliad mix: equal parts of a standard *lime-free* mix and peat moss would serve well. Keep the mix moist, watering moderately throughout the year.

A bit of water-soluble fertilizer should be added to the water in the "vase" once a month.

BOTTLE BRUSH
Callistemon citrinus

The extraordinary bristly bright-red flowers of the aptly-named bottle brush plant have no petals: they are in fact cylindrical clusters of stamens which grow to between 2 and 4 inches in length. The stiff, pointed leaves grow in bunches close to the stem.

These plants will do well if exposed to direct sunlight for several hours a day. Feed and keep them at normal room temperatures in the active growing period. Allow them to rest in winter.

After flowering, bottle brush plants can be cut back quite severely and can stand outside until the nighttime temperature drops below 50°F.

Take heel cuttings in early summer.

CATTLEYA
Cattleya

The hybrid cattleya illustrated here is one of that genus of epiphytic orchids. It has been included here primarily as a reminder or a suggestion of ways in which to extend your range as a grower of indoor flowering plants.

The genus cattleya comprises an enormous number of species and hybrids offering a breathtaking variety of incomparably beautiful flowers.

Readers interested in growing orchids are advised to consult specialist books on the subject and/or to join a society of orchid growers.

COCKSCOMB
Celosia cristata

The yellow, crimson or orange flowers form curious velvety-looking "cockscombs," which last indoors for several weeks in the summer – provided they receive 3 or 4 hours direct sunlight a day.

Use a standard potting mix and keep it constantly moist. Cockscombs will grow to between 1 and 2 feet tall and should be discarded after flowering. Grow new plants from seed.

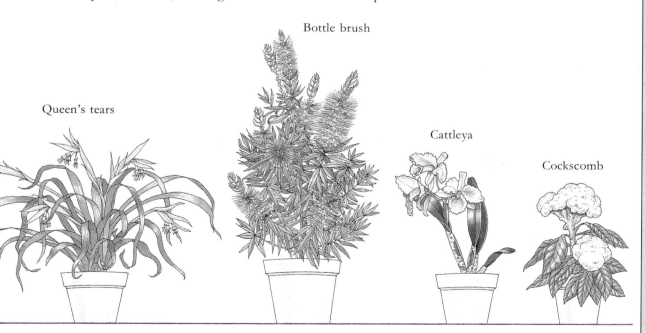

Queen's tears

Bottle brush

Cattleya

Cockscomb

A close-up on bromeliads

Bromeliads are natives of tropical South America and the southern United States. They have become adapted to life in a wide range of habitats – and this is broadly reflected in their physical appearance. Some grow as epiphytes in the branches of trees and have upright rosettes of leaves which form "vases" or reservoirs for catching water as well as other airborne organic debris which forms the basis of the plant's nutritional needs.

Bromeliads which grow more conventionally on the forest floor have flatter, more open rosettes: typical of these are the star shaped members of the genus cryptanthus. Other terrestrial bromeliads found growing on rocks or in crevices in warm, open situations may possess vicious spikes. These act as highly effective protection against browsing animals. The best known member of this group, and the only bromeliad to be exploited com-mercially on a large scale, is the pineapple (*Ananas comosus*).

Other bromeliads, such as the dyckias, have adapted to desert conditions, while still others manage to exist solely on air – extracting and using whatever moisture or nourishing microscopic particles it brings their way.

Most of the bromeliads that are grown as houseplants are epiphytes when growing in the wild. The most popular genera include *Aechmea, Billbergia, Guzmania, Tillandsia* and *Vriesea*. Popular non-epiphytes include members of the genera *Ananas, Cryptanthus* and *Neoregelia*.

Species within these popular houseplant genera display an enormous variety of leaf shapes and formations, but they may be broadly divided into those with rather unimpressive loose rosettes of narrow leaves, as possessed by some tillandsias and billbergias (plants grown mainly for their flowers), and those prized as much for their displays of foliage as for their flowers. In such bromeliads tightly packed clumps of strikingly marked leaves grow in a rosette shape, overlapping at the base to form the central "vase."

Often, the spectacular show of color in many "flowering" bromeliads is not due to the flowers themselves. These are often insignificant. Instead it is the splendid red or pink bracts from which the flowers emerge that form the plant's focus of attraction.

As a general rule, bromeliad vases must always be kept topped up with water and potting mix should always be well-aerated and easy-draining. (See pages 10–11 and 67.)

Building a bromeliad collection is an absorbing and satisfying hobby. As your interest expands, specialist nurseries should be able to meet your needs for less common species.

Guzmania

Vriesea

Tillandsia

Seed propagation

Many flowering houseplants can be propagated from seed, and in the case of flowering annuals, this is the only method possible. Seed is also now available for a number of indoor foliage plants.

It is always best to obtain seed from a reputable mail order company or from a reliable local merchant. Once you have obtained good-quality seeds the observation of certain simple procedures when sowing them will help ensure successful germination.

Seeds vary from tiny, dustspeck-size seeds of begonias and calceolarias to large, hard avocado pits. Some companies "pellet" seeds or give them a hard outer coating for easier handling. This coating is water soluble and will disperse when the seeds receive their first watering. Seeds with a naturally hard coat may need to be lightly "nicked" before planting in order to germinate. The instructions on the packet will usually indicate whether or not this is necessary. If it is, take a sharp knife and, with gentle sawing motions, make a small cut through the seed's outer coat; it is essential that internal tissues are not damaged. All seeds over $\frac{1}{4}$ inch in diameter should be soaked in warm water for 24 hours before sowing.

The very finest seed should simply be scattered on the surface of the rooting mix and left uncovered. Fine seed that is visible may be covered with a light sprinkling of sieved potting mix or milled sphagnum moss. Cover larger seeds with a layer of rooting mix equal to their own thickness.

While seeds may be planted in virtually any container, it is preferable to choose one that is shallow (to prevent heat loss through the mix) and made of plastic (to prevent moisture loss). Beside moisture, seeds need warmth, particularly from below, to germinate. This may be supplied by heating pads of insulated rubber, or by highly sophisticated indoor propagators with thermostatically controlled heating units as well as humidifiers. Whatever container is used, make sure that both it and the rooting medium are sterile.

Label and date all containers.

SOWING SEEDS Step by step

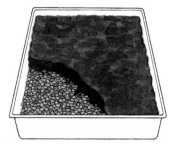

1 Cover the bottom of a shallow plastic container with a layer of gravel. Then add sterilized rooting mix.

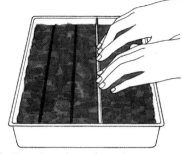

2 Use the edge of a ruler or a piece of card to make shallow furrows. Seeds planted in these will be easier to prick out.

3 Sprinkle fine seeds as thinly and evenly as possible along each furrow. Plant larger seeds at least 1 inch apart.

4 Give the seeds the finest possible misting before covering the pan with a sheet of glass.

5 Keep seeds warm and dark until they germinate. When this happens give them good light (not direct sun) and keep them well ventilated.

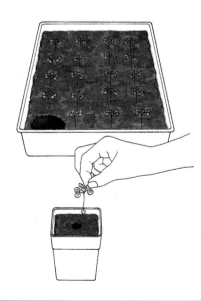

6 Thin seedlings out (leave space equal to their height between them). When 3 pairs of true leaves have formed transplant, holding by seed leaves, if present.

Index of Latin names

Index of English names

Acknowledgments

Publisher — **Bruce Marshall**

Creative Director — **John Bigg**

Editor — **Anne Kilborn**

Managing Editor — **Ruth Binney**

Art Editor — **Pauline Faulks**

Contributors — **Alison Abel / Don Binney**

Text Editing — **Jinny Johnson**

Picture Editor — **Zilda Tandy**

Production Coordination — **Barry Baker / Janice Storr**

Torstar Books Inc.
41 Madison Avenue
Suite 2900
New York, NY 10010

Marshall Editions, an editorial group that specializes in the design and publication of practical and scientific subjects for the general reader, prepared this book in collaboration with ICA-förlaget AB, Sweden. Marshall has written and illustrated standard works on gardening, cookery, needlecraft, photography, biology and technology which are recommended for schools and libraries, as well as for popular reference.

Series Consultant — **Maggie Oster** is advisor to *The Complete Gardening Guide* and has written extensively on the subjects of plants and gardens. She was a major contributor to the *Time-Life Encyclopedia of Gardening* and from 1982–83 was producer and presenter of the monthly television show "Maggie's Garden" on WLKY-TV.

Photographs — Cover photograph Spike Powell
Photograph pp. 2–3 Spike Powell
All other photography courtesy ICA-förlaget AB

Artwork — pp. 6, 8, 10, 12, 24, 35, 54, 57, 62 Norman Bancroft-Hunt
pp. 64–69 Karen Daws/John Craddock ACA
Endpapers Hayward and Martin

Plants and containers — Plants: cover, pp. 2–3 Longmans Ltd